RSF is a simple technique that yields powerful results.

—Kelly Hall-Tompkins, award-winning, Grammy-nominated violin soloist; the "Fiddler," Bartlett Sher Broadway production of *Fiddler on the Roof*; and Founder and Executive/Artistic Director, Music Kitchen–Food for the Soul

RSF has become our operational default system to deal with the unanticipated issues that arise daily.

—Dan Rivers, Managing Partner, Northwestern Mutual

I've always been a results-oriented leader. I often know what I want done but do not convey it in a way that translates. The way I try to improve a situation has always been to point out what is wrong. Doing that can certainly be received as negative when it's not meant to be. RSF helped me think differently, so my message comes across to people in a clearer, more concise, and more positive way.

—Michael Staenberg, President, The Staenberg Group

RSF has been the difference maker for my business. Through the use of RSF, I've been able to overcome hurdles and disrupt industries that were stuck in the Stone Age. For anyone looking to break out and unleash their success, RSF is the way to go!

—Randall S. Boll, CFP, ChFC, CLU, CRPS, CLTC, TEP, ABA, CAP, MSFS, Founder and Chief Vision Officer, TBH Tax LLC

Learning to adopt an RSF mentality was a light switch moment in my life. Challenges in your business and personal life can be overcome and greater confidence built by using Relentless Solution Focus.

—Adam Chustz, Senior Vice President, Stifel Investments

Relentless Solution Focus has been my fulcrum for growth and that of those I lead. Jason taught me that what you focus on expands. Focusing on solutions, not the problem, has freed me to maximize who I am meant to be and embrace the challenge of doing so.

—Kurt M. Dorner, Managing Director, Northwestern Mutual

I have used my time with Jason and Ellen to motivate myself and my team and to passionately discover new possibilities. Since adopting RSF into my daily thinking, I've written two books, continued to build companies, and enjoyed many creative pursuits that come from being open to learning more every day. Dig in, my friend.

—NORTY COHEN, Founder and CEO, Moosylvania, and author of *The Participation Game* and *Join the Brand*

Read this book! Jason's approach to mental toughness and developing a Relentless Solution Focus mindset has improved my personal and professional life. More importantly, our leadership team has embraced RSF with fantastic results. There is always a solution!

—CHRIS SEALS, President, Fraley and Schilling, Inc.

You can't change your destination overnight, but you can change your direction. RSF gives you all the tools you need to start going in this new direction with 100 percent confidence!

—SHANNON BAHRKE HAPPE, Founder, Team Empower Hour, and Olympic silver and bronze medalist in mogul skiing

RELENTLESS
SOLUTION
FOCUS

RELENTLESS SOLUTION FOCUS

TRAIN YOUR MIND TO CONQUER STRESS, PRESSURE, AND UNDERPERFORMANCE

Dr. Jason Selk

Dr. Ellen Reed

New York   Chicago   San Francisco   Athens   London   Madrid
Mexico City   Milan   New Delhi   Singapore   Sydney   Toronto

2 3 4 5 6 7 8 9   LCR   25 24 23 22 21

ISBN   978-1-260-46011-7
MHID   1-260-46011-8

e-ISBN   978-1-260-46012-4
e-MHID   1-260-46012-6

Library of Congress Cataloging-in-Publication Data

Names: Selk, Jason, author.
Title: Relentless solution focus : train your mind to conquer stress,
   pressure, and underperformance / Dr. Jason Selk, with Dr. Ellen Reed.
Description: New York : McGraw Hill, [2020] | Includes bibliographical
   references and index.
Identifiers: LCCN 2020025406 (print) | LCCN 2020025407 (ebook) | ISBN
   9781260460117 (hardback) | ISBN 9781260460124 (ebook)
Subjects: LCSH: Problem solving. | Mental discipline. | Performance. |
   Success.
Classification: LCC HD30.29 .S45 2020 (print) | LCC HD30.29 (ebook) |
   DDC 153.4/3—dc23
LC record available at https://lccn.loc.gov/2020025406
LC ebook record available at https://lccn.loc.gov/2020025407

McGraw Hill books are available at special quantity discounts to use as premiums and sales promotions or for use in corporate training programs. To contact a representative, please visit the Contact Us pages at www .mhprofessional.com.

In loving memory of Mary Scheeler,
who brings the light and color to rainbows,
and to Mark McLean: may others try to live up
to your standard of ferocious selflessness

The mind is everything. What you think you become.
—**BUDDHA**

CONTENTS

PART I

RECOGNIZE
Don't Start a Fight Wearing a Blindfold

PART II

REPLACE
If It's Broken, Fix It

PART III

RETRAIN

When You Train, You Win

Fighting Normal

by Dr. Ellen Reed

Waking up first thing in the morning to my heart racing was familiar and normal for me. "What stressful events do I have on the agenda for the upcoming day? Am I prepared? Did I get enough work done yesterday? Is there anything wrong with my health? What about my family's health? Did I say anything the day before that I regret?"

Some version of these thoughts would swirl through my head before I even realized they were there. This would happen before I opened my eyes, before my body had even recognized it was awake. I was living every day like I was completing a checklist. If I made it through the day without something bad happening, I breathed a sigh of relief—until the next morning.

My focus was primarily on avoiding problems. That focus on *avoiding* problems kept my focus squarely on *problems*. I didn't even consider this an issue. In fact, this is the way the human brain is designed to work. In that sense, this is normal and common.

Normal, in this case, is not a good thing.

My natural state is to wake up in the morning and go through my laundry list of what could potentially go wrong. I know this because I lived this way for most of my life. Don't get me wrong, I wasn't miserable. I wasn't depressed. I was usually successful at most anything I put effort into doing. I would often catch myself thinking, "I'll relax once x is over," or "I'll really be able to enjoy myself after I get through y." I probably could have gone on like this and made it through very successfully on paper—but one day I realized I could look back at my whole life and think, "That went really well, but why couldn't I *truly* enjoy it?"

I often think of my two grandfathers—my two "Papaws." My mom's dad, Thomas Bryant, died when he was 83. On his deathbed, he was surrounded by his entire family. I watched my grandmother—his wife, Patricia, of close to 65 years—hold him and tell him that she loved him, that it was OK for him to go. It was one of the most touching and important moments I've ever witnessed. He was the first person I lost in my life, and although we all wish we had more time with him, I used to think, "Papaw Bryant really won the game." While I'm sure he had his share of struggles, nothing tremendously "bad" happened to him. He didn't have to bury a spouse, and his children were all healthy and thriving at the time of his death. He was a grandfather and a great-grandfather—he had a long life as a true patriarch to a wonderful family.

My dad's father, John Hinkel Sr., died on his eighty-ninth birthday. His death was sudden but not unexpected, and our family was able to say good-bye to him. My siblings and cousins who lived out of town connected over an app on our phones, and my dad held the phone so we could watch our Papaw Hinkel receive his last rites, and each could say good-bye to him—another experience for which I am incredibly grateful. Just before I was born, he lost his first wife, Naomi, of 30 years, my grandmother, to cancer. His second wife of 32 years, Joanne, suffered from late-stage Alzheimer's, and he spent years taking care of her in their home until he fell and broke his hip. At that point, it became clear that she needed full-time care that he no longer could provide. He was devoted to her until the end, as painful as it must have been to watch her memory and abilities fade away. When he was 87, his son, my uncle Mark, was killed tragically by a drunk driver—an insurmountable loss to our family. My grandfather watched both of his beloved spouses suffer terrible diseases. He buried a spouse and a child. Those experiences are about as bad as it gets.

Two patriarchs of loving families who lived long, full lives, both surrounded by their families on their deathbeds. I can't imagine that either went through his list of bad things that happened to determine how he felt about his life at the end. Regardless of the amount of suffering each endured, I like to think that both my grandfathers were taking in all the beauty and love of their families surrounding them when they passed. When I look forward, it is easy to be consumed with how much bad could potentially lurk in the future, but when I picture both my grandfathers in their final moments, I can't imagine either of them focusing on anything but the good in his life—as there was so much of it. Why waste the whole life part worrying about the potential bad when I just don't think it will matter in the end?

Holding my breath waiting for a potential problem to arise or for a present complication to go away was neither fulfilling nor necessary, yet this is the way most of us go through life.

In terms of mental toughness, I would categorize my natural state (without any commitment to mental training) as pretty typical. Unfortunately, being typical puts people at a pretty high propensity for anxiety, worry, and underperformance. The human brain is designed to search for potential problems. We are designed this way for an important reason. From an evolutionary standpoint, there is no denying that it is important to quickly recognize the bear running at you in the woods or the car racing toward you traveling the wrong direction. We recognize potential problems quickly. That's the good news. The bad news is that this wreaks havoc on our health, happiness, and success. But it doesn't have to.

I was very fortunate to start working with Dr. Jason Selk 15 years ago. We happened to cross paths when I was in graduate school studying psychology and taking as many dance classes and opportunities as I could get my hands on. Jason needed someone to help with administrative tasks, and I needed a part-time job during school. As an aspiring dancer studying psychology, the merging of psychology with the fundamentals of achieving peak performance was the perfect fit for me. He was about to begin his role as the director of mental training for the St. Louis Cardinals, and he knew his business was about to explode. He was right. Four bestselling books later, Jason developed the fundamentals of Relentless Solution Focus (RSF), the mind's ability to stay focused on solutions, especially in the face of adversity. These fundamentals have helped countless individuals lead better lives and reach their own ultimate levels of success. No person is more grateful for these fundamentals than I. Adopting an RSF mindset changed the way I experience life.

Alongside Jason, I teach and work with people on developing the fundamentals of mental toughness on a daily basis. In addition to my career as a performance coach, I have now been a professional dancer for more than 10 years. A typical day for me begins with five-plus hours of dance class and rehearsals before transitioning into coaching my athlete and business clients, while being a wife and a mom.

"Performing" isn't limited to being on stage in front of hundreds or thousands of people. We all perform constantly throughout the day, and mental toughness is the way to achieve optimal performance, no matter the arena. Whether I'm performing on the phone with a client, in a rehearsal or daily technique class, as a wife and mom, or on an actual stage, these mental toughness fundamentals have been integral in helping me work to achieve my potential—and more importantly, truly enjoy the process.

THE "RELENTLESS" IN RELENTLESS SOLUTION FOCUS

For a while, I thought I was doing fairly well maintaining an RSF mindset. For the most part, I would sail through my negative thoughts and problems and on to solution-focused thinking. Every day wasn't perfect, but my natural state had shifted from one of constant worry to one of contentment and optimism. I was waking up excited about the day without the racing heart and the immediate subtle feeling of anxiety.

Then I became a mom.

After my first son, William, was born, I felt like I made up for all the lost time that I had not spent in a constant state of anxiety over the past several years. When it came to worrying about my son, all bets were off. I used the excuse that when it came to him, it just wasn't possible to not allow myself to "go there." That just came with the territory of being a mom. Moms worry. That is what I would tell myself. I did a really good job of talking myself out of having to commit to RSF. That free pass for problem-focused thoughts I gave myself for my son found its way into other areas of my life, as problem-focused thinking tends to do.

I should note that there wasn't even really anything to worry about. My son and family were thriving. It didn't matter. When left to its own devices, worry for me does not care that there is "nothing to worry about." My brain is good at finding something to worry about. Most brains are good at this. Actually, sometimes the fact that there was nothing to worry about was exactly what I would worry about. "What if something changes? When is the other shoe going to drop? There has to be something negative waiting around the corner. . . ."

My own career and my work with athletes and professionals in the business world has taught me that you don't need to be running a multimillion-dollar business, you don't need to be playing Game 7 of the World Series, you don't need to be at the free-throw line with three seconds left, you don't need to be on a stage in front of an audience for pervasive worry, pressure, and negativity to be common. In fact, the *easiest* arena for me to apply the RSF mindset is in my professional dancing career, which most people would assume might carry with it a great deal of pressure. It's with the more common day-to-day life pressures that I find myself having to work harder at maintaining mental toughness. And like it or not, the mental weakness of negative thoughts in even one area has major implications on how you experience all areas of your life.

It took a while for me to become aware that my racing heart-beat during my first moments of consciousness in the mornings had returned. It felt so familiar that I didn't immediately notice the toll it was taking on me.

I had been failing at RSF, and I had the racing heartbeat to thank for showing me. I finally recognized that my excuse of being a mom was just that—an excuse. I was back to square one in terms of maintaining an RSF mindset. Well, to be fair, probably closer to square two, given that I was still helping *other* people commit to RSF. I *knew* the fundamentals backward and forward. That should count for something, right?

It doesn't.

Knowing Something Isn't Enough— You Must Do Something

You can talk about it, read about it, teach it all day long, and *know* what you should be doing, but mental toughness requires that you actually *do* something. In this book, we will guide you through the fundamentals of adopting an RSF mindset—the ulti-mate measure of mental toughness.

I am good at my job of coaching others largely because men-tal toughness is not natural for me. It is likely not natural for you either. Mental toughness is not supposed to be easy. It comes more easily to some than to others, but it is a discipline that *everyone* has to work to maintain. I have gotten off track at times, but I have fought to get back on. Understanding and committing to the fight is a crucial part of RSF.

The key to RSF is the *Relentless* part. It demands commitment. It requires relentlessness because there are times when you will not want to focus on finding a solution, when you will not even recognize that you are focusing on a problem, when it'll be easier to give in to your negative thoughts. And just when you get good at it, something will come along and challenge you. Life has a way of doing that.

Your brain is designed for you to experience mental weakness—it is likely very normal for you, as it was for me. Mental toughness is not natural. These facts make it easy for people to accept their natural state, but you can *learn* to become mentally tough. And by "learn," I mean understand the fundamentals, execute them on a daily basis, fight to maintain them, and then work to get them back when you fail. It won't be easy, but you can do it, and we will show you how. There is no greater gift to yourself and to those you love for improved health, happiness, and success than to read this book and commit to the RSF mindset.

Some days, you'll fail. Mental toughness is not about being perfect. That is important enough to say again—Mental toughness is not about being perfect. It is about having and practicing the tools to fight back when you (or life) are not perfect. There is no end point to mental toughness. Mental toughness is about the fight. It's about knowing this game doesn't end. "Winning" is temporary, and sometimes it means losing "better" than you would have had you not fought. I guarantee that the results will be worth all of the losing battles. It is in the battles that you learn to fight your normal and win.

INTRODUCTION

You Are Worth It

by Dr. Jason Selk

What if I told you that we could cut mental health disorders in half and reduce the amount of disease and physical ailments in the world by 30 percent? How about if I said that what you are about to learn in this book is the secret to gaining control in your life and to significantly increasing your happiness, success, and ability to perform under pressure? And that what was required takes only three minutes daily?

Think about that for a moment. You can literally cut in half the likelihood you will suffer from depression and anxiety. You can also decrease by 30 percent the likelihood of having a major disease. You will be measurably more successful, and it only requires three minutes per day of effort. What you are about to read may very well be the most important thing you ever learn.

This book will equip you with the knowledge and training required to unlock the *true* secret of human happiness, health, and success. The first thing you must understand before reading any further is that you are worth it. You are worthy of being happy, you are worthy of being healthy, and you are worthy of performing at a higher level than you already are. No matter where you come from, what you have done in the past, or what you do in the present, you deserve joy and peace and contentment in life. I will say it again: *You are worth it.*

Just how powerful is the mind? The truth is, no one really knows. The brain is the epicenter of human activity and existence.

Our brains control the way we feel, behave, and experience life. Our thoughts dictate our entire life experience.

Most people spend half their lives worrying about what *could* go wrong and the other half focusing on all that they don't have. In this book you will learn to achieve what you never imagined. And when something does go wrong, you will know how to make it right. No more nights lying in bed, stressing about all of life's potential landmines. Instead, you will have confidence knowing that you are finally in control of your life and can deal with any problem that comes your way.

Over the course of my career as a performance coach, I have been fortunate enough to work with some of the healthiest, happiest, and most successful people walking the planet. In studying thousands of people—CEOs, professional athletes, business owners, religious and industry leaders, celebrated actors and musicians, and others considered to be "the best"—I discovered that the one quality many of these superstar humans have in common is mental toughness. Those who, by all accounts, seemed typical in looks, skills, and intelligence, yet were producing abnormally high results, were the ones who seemed to have mastered the mental side of life.

They possess the uncanny ability to control what goes on between their ears. Instead of allowing their mind to focus on everything they *didn't* have or *couldn't* do, the most successful people have learned to direct their thoughts in a manner that produces positive emotions and productive actions.

Have you ever had the experience of knowing you should do something, yet not do it? You know that taking action would be in your best interest, and your life would be improved; however, somehow you find yourself not getting it done? Of course. We all have. This is actually quite natural. Unfortunately, natural is bad in this case. RSF will strategically teach you to eliminate or significantly decrease the likelihood of "not being in control."

True success boils down to *thought control*. Those who are happiest, healthiest, and most successful *choose* thoughts that biologically improve their quality of life. *Mental toughness is thought control*—choosing the right thoughts that make you feel better and cause you to take action on what creates positive outcomes.

Over the years I have had some clients show up in my office already possessing strength between their ears. Others had to learn and work at it. I found that everyone who worked on training his or her mind to be more mentally tough made progress. Everyone. Mental toughness is the foundation for making better decisions and actually sticking to those decisions.

It isn't just that mentally tough people spend more time thinking. Many people spend countless hours in thought. Mental toughness is different. Mentally tough people are actually *better* at thinking. They are better at making decisions more quickly and with better results. They make more effective decisions about what to say and do, and they follow through more deeply. When mentally tough people do get off track, they can rebound more quickly.

Mentally tough people lower their risk for several major diseases, including cancer, heart disease, stroke, and respiratory disease, and they are far less likely to suffer from anxiety, depression, post-traumatic stress disorder (PTSD), and sleep issues. Mentally tough people are *significantly* happier, healthier, and more successful than most people.

What I've learned, and what I teach and coach together with my colleague Dr. Ellen Reed is that mental toughness is the ability to focus on solutions, especially in the face of adversity. It is the focus on solutions instead of problems that is the key to health and success. As easy as this might sound, it runs completely counter to our nature and is quite difficult. However, with a little education and training, we can overcome the way our minds are wired and achieve mental toughness—and it can be learned by anyone. This is Relentless Solution Focus (RSF), and

Ellen and I teach it to our coaching clients and to the tens of thousands of people in the audiences we speak to each year.

Twenty years ago, I set out to combine what I know about cognitive neuroscience, brain chemistry, and human performance to create a training method to show people exactly *how* to develop mental toughness. After years of research with clinical patients, I developed a three-step process designed to help people change and control their thoughts, feelings, and behaviors through RSF, and it has since been proven to help people win World Series, Super Bowls, national championships, and Olympic gold medals, as well as increase business production by up to 30 percent year over year. More important, this three-step process will make you a better (happier and healthier) person—a measurably improved version of yourself. Take it from business owner Tammy Shadlow:

> It used to be that some days I would be paralyzed with the everyday pressures of work and life. Now, instead of actually letting stress build up, I use RSF to work the negativity out of my system. Instead of waking up and immediately feeling stress and anxiety, I actually wake up every day clearheaded and feel like I am at least one step ahead of where I was yesterday. I am a better leader at work, and no doubt I am more present in my relationships with my husband and children. RSF changed my life, or maybe I should say it gave me my life back.

A current Major League pitcher and Cy Young Winner says:

> I used to be out there on the mound, and all kinds of negative stuff could get into my head—if it was a windy day, or if the guy I was going up against took it to me last time around. It could even be personal stuff—if I had been fighting with my wife or having trouble with one of the kids. All that stuff would get into my head and distract me. Now I bounce that stuff out in 60 seconds or less. RSF is definitely the reason I have continued to have such a strong career, and it definitely helped keep me on track the year I won the Cy Young.

WHY MENTAL TOUGHNESS?

Mental toughness is not about receiving a pep talk; it's a trainable skill set. When it comes to mental toughness, there are two goals. First, it is essential for high-level performers to be able to deal with adversity when it strikes. Whether the adversity comes in the form of illness, injury, bad weather, or any of life's other mishaps, individuals need to be able to overcome obstacles and perform. This all begins with the thoughts in your head. Typical people focus on the adversity, whereas mentally tough people have learned to zero in on what they can do to overcome the adversity. The RSF mindset enables people to better recognize and prepare for the storms of life, so they not only survive adversity, but actually learn to *thrive* in it.

The second goal of mental toughness is to systematically reduce the amount of negative "head trash" that most people experience. We have somewhere between 12,000 and 60,000 thoughts daily (2005, the National Science Foundation), and 80 percent of those thoughts are negative. Additionally, research has found that of all the negative stuff we think about, 85 percent of it will never happen (Leahy, 2005). Simply put, roughly 70 percent of our daily thoughts are worried about things that will never happen. In everyday life, most people are overwhelmed and inundated with negative thoughts of all the potential problems that could occur. It's normal to think about all of the things that could go wrong only to miss out on all that's going well. Developing mental toughness will significantly reduce the volume of negative thinking, allowing you to attack and win every day, living life to the fullest, while creating the mindset and game plan for high-level success.

RSF is the antidote to mental weakness and negative thinking. When I was working for the St. Louis Rams, I asked the head groundskeeper, Scott Parker, how I could get rid of the weeds in my yard at home. With great confidence, he replied, "Grow more grass." Growing more grass chokes out the weeds. The same is true for the human mind. If we can train ourselves to have more positive thoughts, they will choke out the negative thoughts. The result? Less drama and adversity. If you like drama, you are going to hate RSF. Developing an RSF mindset drains the drama out of life and gives you a distinct advantage at working through adversity. When life becomes difficult, mentally tough people are far more able to solve their problems. They can improve and move forward one problem at a time. Mentally tough people know they are mentally tough. They are acutely aware and in control of their thoughts, and they know they have an advantage over other people because of it.

When a person learns to relentlessly replace each negative thought with a solution, weakness shrinks and strength grows, creating confidence and momentum. If the first solution doesn't solve the problem, there is another solution waiting in the wings. When problems are reduced to a level of insignificance, the human spirit soars, taking individuals to higher levels of performance, health, and achievement.

We have all heard by now how important it is to be positive. For years, researchers such as Martin Seligman (father of optimism) and Carol Dweck (author of *Mindset*) have warned us about the performance issues and health concerns associated with negativity and pessimism. Why then is being positive so difficult? It's because no one has taught us how to retrain our brain.

TRAINING FOR RSF AND MENTAL TOUGHNESS

RSF is a concrete and proven three-step process that *trains*, not teaches, people to achieve mental toughness and control over their thoughts, emotions, and performance.

1. **Recognize:** The first step in the RSF process is learning to recognize when negative thinking has set in. As easy as it sounds, self-assessment is actually quite difficult. We are biologically wired to focus on our problems. The good news is that we all have a built-in alarm system that literally screams at us when negative thoughts have set in. Unfortunately, very few people have learned how to recognize this alarm. RSF teaches people exactly how to recognize the onset of mental weakness and negative thinking and to effectively use it to create positive behavior change.

2. **Replace:** Once an individual has learned to recognize problem-focused thoughts, it is essential to replace the negative thinking with more positive thoughts. The key is to do this quickly—within 60 seconds or less. This simple tool in the form of a question guarantees the replacement of problem-centric thought (PCT) with an RSF mindset: *What is one thing I can do right now that could make this better?*

3. **Retrain:** No muscle becomes strong without training, and the brain is a muscle somewhat like the bicep. Developing mental strength requires training. Although negative thinking is hardwired into all of us, neuroplasticity (the ability of the brain to change) proves that individuals can actually retrain themselves to be significantly more solution-focused and positive, rather than defaulting to the usual emphasis on problems and negativity. You will first develop your framework for success by determining your life's vision and what you need to do on a daily basis to achieve that vision. And you will learn the two proven tools (Mental Workout and Success Log) that will train your mind for the RSF required to conquer stress, pressure, and

underperformance. The training requires no more than three minutes a day.

Throughout the book, we will be asking you to do some exercises, and the templates for these are available for download at relentlesssolutionfocus.com. Let's begin right here, right now, with you. And allow me to say it again so that you never forget: *You are worth it.*

PART I

RECOGNIZE

Don't Start a Fight
Wearing a Blindfold

1

PCT

The Greatest Obstacle
to Mental Toughness

Let's start with a very important question: Are you a pessimist or an optimist? On a daily basis do you find yourself worrying and talking about potential problems, or do you find yourself naturally thinking about all of your blessings and the good in the world?

Most pessimists don't like to admit to being pessimistic. The most common argument I hear from pessimists is, "I am not a pessimist. I just like to be prepared for what could go wrong." If that argument sounds familiar, you're probably a pessimist. Optimists tend to believe that "in the end, everything will work out."

By nature each of us has pessimistic and optimistic qualities. I would no more want you to abandon thoughts about all those good things in life as I would want you not to realize that sometimes bad things happen. The good news is that you are about to learn exactly what you can do to channel your current levels of pessimism and optimism into a mindset that combines the positive qualities of both to create a much more effective way to experience life. That is the Relentless Solution Focus (RSF) mindset.

People with RSF have learned to keep a positive outlook with the understanding that things could go wrong. Instead of worrying about the potential mishaps, they assume all is well until the problem actually presents itself. And when problems do become a reality, people with RSF attack their problems with solutions. Sounds great, right? It *is* great. The only issue is that it takes some work to consistently execute on this new way of thinking.

People with RSF attack their problems with solutions.

I want to take a moment to talk about what this book will *not* do. This book will not teach you to become an unrealistic optimist or someone who views life through rose-colored glasses, thinking that no matter what, everything will work out for the best. Nor will this be a place where you get permission to consistently "borrow trouble," to think about potential problems that often never materialize.

Being pessimistic is quite common. A person may have concerns about a hundred things that *could* go wrong, when in reality, only two or three will actually occur. Unfortunately, our brains and our nervous systems have a very difficult time telling the difference between what we *think* will happen and reality. Imagining all those potential problems can become its own reality.

Our brains have a difficult time telling the difference between what we think will happen and reality.

Being prepared for all those potential problems has caused us as a society to become ill. Our society is collectively sick with problem-centric thought (PCT), and, unfortunately, it can be deadly. Now more than ever, we are underperforming on our individual and collective potential. There is an abundance of incompetence, hatred, and pain in our world. Negativity is commonplace. We are losing our way, and in large part, this is due to PCT. PCT is the biological tendency for the human mind to focus on the negative. Simply put, our brains are wired to focus on problems. These problems can come in the form of what you think you screwed up that day, what you feel like you are still lacking in life, or any potential problem that could exist.

Problem-centric thought: the biological tendency to focus on problems or the negative

As our species evolved, a focus on survival was critical. Life-ending threats from other humans or from nature were often imminent, and resources were scarce. It was much more costly for our species to assume that there *wasn't* a potential threat lurking in the woods than to assume that there was. This bias toward focusing on problems and expecting the worst was necessary to avoid critical mistakes that would cost lives. This is how our brains evolved to what they are today, and this negativity or problem bias still exists. Now that our environment is much more stable and resources are much more plentiful, PCT limits our potential and increases stress, pressure, and underperformance.

The most difficult part of being mentally tough is actually being able to recognize PCT when it happens. Negative thinking floods the human mind on such a consistent basis that PCT is practically invisible to most people. No matter how tough you are, getting into a fistfight wearing a blindfold is a *very* bad idea. There is one simple reason for this: it's awfully hard to hit what you can't see.

Think about how your typical day goes. You do 99 things right, but maybe one thing doesn't go perfectly. What does your mind have a tendency to focus on? If you are like most people, your mind dwells on that one imperfection. That is PCT, and it is the exact opposite of RSF. Everyone has a natural tendency toward PCT. It's completely normal. The human brain is wired this way. But it has a significant negative impact on your quality of life and ability to perform at a high level.

Think of PCT as a constant drip of water falling every second, minute after minute, day after day, year after year, on the same point on the roof of your home. Over time, that consistent drip breaks down the shingles on your roof and eventually begins wearing through the wood and into the drywall of the ceiling. Once this occurs, it won't take long before your entire house begins to break down. The damage that incessant drip causes is the equivalent of the impact of PCT over time on a person's quality of life. PCT erodes the human spirit. It robs us of our happiness and hope, and it causes good people to make bad decisions and choices. PCT may be the single greatest destructive force in the history of our species.

Just because PCT is typical and not your fault doesn't mean that you cannot or should not do anything about it. Let's be clear. This book is not just about knowing or understanding; it's about *doing*. You are going to learn how to do what is necessary to make positive change. You will learn exactly what the best in the world do to overcome PCT and develop mental toughness.

We want you to think about mental toughness as a fight, a fight against PCT. In the first three chapters you will learn how to take the blindfold off and more clearly recognize when PCT is beginning to push you around.

Mental toughness is a fight against PCT.

MENTAL WEAKNESS AFFECTS US ALL

Potential for greatness and actual greatness are two very different things. Potential refers to what may come if all goes well. True greatness happens when a person learns to "get it done," no matter what the circumstance. Sadly, everything going just as planned is quite rare. A major part of developing mental toughness is understanding that life often does not go as you'd hoped. Greatness lies in the hands of those rare few who know how to thrive in the face of adversity. Realizing that things will and do go wrong is an essential part of being able to recognize PCT.

The point we want to make right off the bat is that everyone needs to fight against PCT and mental weakness. Mental weakness is natural—it affects us all—and it can defeat us if we don't learn how to see it when it is happening.

Realizing that things will and do go wrong is an essential part of being able to recognize PCT.

Saying that Alfonso Soriano achieved greatness is an understatement. Soriano began his professional baseball career in 1996 in Hiroshima. He was signed by the Yankees to play in the minor league in 1998, and he was named most valuable player (MVP) in the All-Star Futures Game in 1999 after hitting two home runs. He made his first appearance in Major League Baseball (MLB) with the Yankees later that year. He became the second Yankee in franchise history to hit 30 home runs and have 30 stolen bases in 2002, a feat that he repeated the following year. In 2003, he finished among the top five in the league for base hits, doubles, stolen bases, and home runs, and he led the league in at bats. Soriano experienced continued success over the next several years playing for the Texas Rangers and the Washington Nationals, and then he landed with the Chicago Cubs after signing an eight-year $136 million contract—the largest in Cubs' franchise history at the time. He was on fire.

In 2013, he was traded back to the New York Yankees. In his first months as a returning Yankee, he broke his personal record for runs batted in (RBIs) in a game—twice. First batting in six runs, and then beating his own record the following day by batting in seven. Alfonso Soriano knew a lot about success over the course of his career, and there was no end in sight—until PCT got a firm hold on him.

In July 2014, Soriano was released from the Yankees after playing only 67 games. How does someone as wildly successful as he hit a slump worthy of derailing a 16-year career? PCT. After 16 years of success, what was on Soriano's mind at the end of his career was what was *not* working. So much so that he couldn't get himself out of this mindset. So much so that he retired having "lost the love and passion to play the game."

In the months leading up to his release, Soriano was vocal about what was going on in his mind:

> . . . When the team is struggling . . . that makes it worse because . . . I'm frustrated the way we are struggling. . . . I feel more pressure because the team is struggling . . . It's not good to think that way. It makes it worse. But you cannot control your mind. Sometimes your mind controls your body, but you cannot control your mind. . . . Most of the time now, I'm not putting the ball in play, so that makes me more anxious and more angry.

When reporters asked if he remembered being this lost in the past, he replied: "No, no, no . . . I think this is the worst . . . I've had a lot of bad habits in my career, but I don't remember one like this." He couldn't get his mind off the fact that he wasn't hitting and the fact that his team was struggling. The more interviews he did about his slump, the more it reinforced the problem-focused mindset and derailed his confidence. When you are focused on your problems, and everyone is talking to you about the problems you are having, it's quite likely your problems will grow. Think about it: If everyone is telling you that you are in a slump, and you are telling yourself that you are in the worst slump you've ever had, what chance do you have of coming out of it? The odds are certainly not in your favor.

On November 4, 2014, Soriano announced his retirement: "I've lost the love and passion to play the game. . . . Although I consider myself to be in great shape, my mind is not focused on baseball." For years, Soriano was seemingly superhuman. What happened at the end of his career paints an unfortunate picture of the impact PCT can have on human performance.

Let me give you another example of how common PCT is. My brother has taught me many lessons in life, the most valuable of which was just how pervasive PCT is. He had a unique way of making me fully appreciate something that I often completely took for granted. One time, he bear-hugged me in the pool, submerging me under the water, pulling me up just long enough to catch one breath, and then dunking me back down again. In that moment, I appreciated just how valuable oxygen was.

Oxygen, in fact, is the most valuable resource to our species. While society puts a higher dollar value on gold and diamonds, oxygen is much more valuable than money, jewels, or any other resource known to our species. We would die very quickly without it.

Consider the last time you thought to yourself while taking a breath, "This is great! I have an abundance of the most valuable resource known to our species, and I don't even have to work that hard to get it!" For me, it required being repeatedly submerged in the pool that day to increase my appreciation.

Oxygen is the most valuable resource on Earth, yet we rarely, if ever, focus on the fact that we have an abundance of it. What probably does come easily to you is focusing on what you *don't* have an abundance of. Think about the last time you thought to yourself, "I don't have enough money," "I don't have enough respect," "I don't have enough love," "I don't have enough time," "I don't have enough . . . (you fill in the blank)." My guess is you probably don't need to look back much further than the past few hours to find an instance when you recognized or complained about something you *don't* have.

Let's try a little exercise. Look around you right now. Whether you are sitting in an office, driving in your car, or lying in bed, look around you and take note of what you see. Most people, especially when doing this for the first time, zero in on imperfections. For example, I am sitting in my home office right now. As I look out the window, I see my deck with outdoor furniture and beyond, hundreds of trees in the distance. Although I have done this exercise before, my eyes are still drawn to the one outdoor chair on my deck that blew over in last night's windstorm. At first glance, I totally overlook the fact that nine chairs made it through last night's upheaval. It is also easy to miss the beauty of the deck (it is only two years old and looks really good) or how fortunate I am to have a deck in the first place.

When you allow yourself to look at life through the normal, problem-focused lens, you cause yourself to see and feel more negativity. I assure you, when you remove the problem lens, you will be shocked at how much good there is in your life and in the world. RSF is not about learning to look through rose-colored glasses, but rather learning to see the world and your life experience through accurately focused lenses. Of course there is pain and suffering in the world, and there is a certain brutality to life that all of us experience; however, there is also so very much greatness in ourselves and in the world that we often overlook because of PCT. RSF is all about being a realist *and* a winner. Instead of only seeing the problems, you will learn to first see the good and then to be relentless about improving any circumstances you are not happy with. The impact of adopting RSF is nothing short of extreme.

RSF is not about learning to look through rose-colored glasses, but rather learning to see the world and your life experience through accurately focused lenses.

HELPING EACH OTHER GET
BETTER AT . . . BEING WORSE

Unfortunately, because we are all built with the PCT tendency, we feed off one another, and our focus on problems fuels more problems. Read the newspaper or watch the news. The large majority of the coverage is focused on problems. Rarely do you see or hear about a solution. Your average 90-minute movie devotes about 95 percent (or more) to presenting a myriad of problems and usually only a handful of minutes to the solution. In fact, arriving at a solution is usually a pretty good indication that the movie is close to over. When you hang around the watercooler or coffee machine, people are likely not discussing how great management is or how lucky they are to be able to show up to work every day. You will likely overhear a laundry list of complaints or problems. The next time you are in a meeting, take mental note of how much time is spent discussing problems. Problems, unfortunately, are how we relate to each other. Because we relate to each other this way, we become better at being worse.

An exception to this might be the photos people display on social media of their smiling, vacation-filled, heavily filtered lives. But take a moment to reflect on your thought process when you are scrolling though Instagram. Are your thoughts typically, "Look how joyful and beautiful they all look. I'm so happy for them." Or are they more typically, "Why can I not afford to go on a tropical vacation?" or "If only I looked as young as she does," or "I wish my marriage was as happy and easy as theirs." While you may *want* to be happy for other people's successes that you see on social media, PCT is often the first instinct. This is why social media can so often leave people feeling depressed and inadequate.

PCT derailed Alfonso Soriano's confidence and focus, and he wasn't able to finish his career the way he wanted. Don't get me wrong, he experienced great success over most of it, and his accomplishments are nothing short of superstar quality, but PCT undeniably played a huge role in his release and retirement, not to mention his loss of love and passion for the game. PCT didn't care that he had earned $157 million or made seven All-Star teams throughout his career. No matter how many records he had broken or how many millions he had earned, Soriano couldn't get his focus off how his team was struggling or how badly he needed to get a hit. The more he thought about it, the more it was reinforced. That's how PCT works. Thinking about or focusing on his problems made those problems much worse—to the point of robbing Soriano of his love and passion for a game that had brought him so much success.

We share Alfonso's story to demonstrate the hold that PCT can have even over a person who experienced more success than most people even dream about. PCT doesn't care if you are an MLB ballplayer or an accountant or a stay-at-home mom. It can and will sink its claws into you and won't let go unless you have the tools to fight it.

CAN YOU BECOME MENTALLY TOUGH?

Going through life letting PCT govern your thoughts is like trying to win the big game by playing prevent defense. If you are not a sports fan, prevent defense is a strategy in which the defense attempts to succeed by taking a much more passive approach to guard against all potential problems. This is like playing not to lose instead of playing to win. If there is one thing I have learned about prevent defense, it's that the teams that use it significantly decrease their chances of keeping such a large lead. If you want to win in life, you must stop running from your problems and instead learn to *attack and defeat* them.

PCT is the greatest obstacle to mental toughness, and you can learn to combat it if you believe you can, and you commit to doing so. Two points Soriano made in his statements explain why his problem focus greatly contributed to the end of his career:

1. It is "not good to think that way."
2. He believed he could not control his mind, so he couldn't.

He knew that it was "not good to think that way," but he also believed there was nothing he could do about it. In the words of Henry Ford, "If you think you can do a thing, or think you can't do a thing, you're right."

If you want to win in life, you must stop running from your problems and instead learn to attack and defeat *them.*

While Soriano was right about it not being good to focus on problems or adversity, he was wrong when he said, "You cannot control your mind." If your mind is focused on how long it's been since you've had a hit, or how bad your slump has become, or how badly you need a break, by default it is *not* focused on what you need to be doing to get out of the slump. In the meantime, these negative thoughts are greatly increasing stress and anxiety while crippling confidence. This is a recipe for continued disaster. Your brain can only fully focus on one thing at a time. When problems consume your thoughts, you are closed off to the possibility of solutions, and you easily become lost in a spiral of negativity. Remember, looking through the PCT lens is totally *natural*.

Let's say it again: your mind can fully focus on only one thing at a time, and if you are focused on a problem, then you cannot be focused on the solution. If you believe there is nothing you can do to control your thoughts, then you are absolutely right. If you believe, however, that you can learn to become more mentally tough to combat PCT, then you are also absolutely right. Science proved long ago that a person can indeed learn to control his or her thoughts, and it actually doesn't require much work at all.

Your mind can fully focus on only one thing at a time, and if you are focused on a problem, then you cannot be focused on the solution.

Think about it this way—if you tell yourself you are an A student, but you are currently averaging a D in math, you are going to be uncomfortable with this fact and work your tail off to get your grade up. You may speak with the teacher after class, you may ask for extra-credit opportunities, or you may dedicate more time to study for the upcoming exam. In contrast, if you tell yourself you are lousy at math and are currently making a D, you have no reason to put in the effort to improve at math. Your performance is consistent with your expectations of yourself. By saying you're lousy at math, you've given yourself an excuse not to work at it. Almost everyone that enters our office initially displays some version of this I'm-just-not-good-at-it mentality in one way or another.

Justin, for example, was a top-producing financial advisor I worked with several years ago. He came to me for help to reach the next level, while maintaining a balance with his family. While he had been experiencing greater financial success over the past few years, he had noticed a disconnect with his family. He was productive throughout the day, but he was leaving the office much later than he wanted. He was exhausted when he arrived at home at the end of the day, and he couldn't get his mind off work. He would bide his time until his kids were in bed and then go back to his computer. His relationships with his wife and three kids were suffering, and he was having trouble pushing through to the next level at work.

Justin identified that he needed to get into the office an hour earlier each day to have more uninterrupted time before the rest of his coworkers arrived. He knew this would make a huge difference in the amount of work he would be able to get done at the office. He left our session ready and excited to put his new plan in place.

The next month, he came back in not much of a better position. I asked him how getting into the office an hour earlier was going, and he replied, "It worked great for a few days, but I wasn't able to keep it up. It was too hard to get out of bed in the morning. I'm just not a morning person." I asked him if he felt it was worth it to recommit to that goal, and he said, "Yes, I definitely think it will make a huge difference in my day. I just need to make it happen." He came back to see me the following month, and when I asked how the plan to wake up earlier was going, he again replied with some version of how it was "extra difficult" for him because he was "just not a morning person."

At that point, I gave Justin one rule: he was not allowed to say to himself or to anyone else that he was "not a morning person." Instead, he had to replace that negative thought with "I'm learning to be a morning person."

He had already decided that it was not possible for him to wake up earlier, so it wasn't happening for him, even though he had set a goal for it month after month. His viable excuse was that he "just wasn't a morning person." When he stopped allowing himself to use that excuse, his mind opened up to potential solutions. He realized he needed roughly eight hours of sleep to be ready for the upcoming day. With that in mind, he set a "lights-out curfew" for himself on work nights at 10:00 p.m. so that when his alarm went off at 6:00 the next morning, even if he was initially tired, he would know he had the necessary sleep to make it through the day.

With that one adjustment to his thoughts, Justin started to believe that he *could* get himself to wake up earlier, so he began looking for ways to make it happen. Within six months, he proudly described himself as a morning person. Getting into the office an hour earlier made all the difference for him in terms of his productivity throughout the day. He was able to leave the office roughly two hours earlier, with energy for his family. He was able to change his behaviors to eventually create an impactful change in his life by making one simple change to the way he was thinking.

Alfonso Soriano was right: It's not good to think the way PCT drives us to think. He had every reason to believe in his ability to perform well at the plate given his countless successes, but he still allowed PCT to derail him. My guess is that you likely already knew before picking up this book that focusing on problems is not good for you. That may even be why you picked up this book. You know this, but what do you do about it? Soriano made the mistake of believing there was nothing he could do to control his mind. Mental toughness can be learned, but you have to do some work to get there.

The first step in developing mental toughness is learning to recognize when PCT is becoming your focus. Recognizing PCT gives you the opportunity to do something about it.

The first step in developing mental toughness is learning to recognize when PCT is becoming your focus.

KNOWING SOMETHING
DOES NOTHING . . .

My good friend and business partner Tom Bartow says often, "Knowing something doesn't do anything to change your life; doing something does." Although *knowing* is the first step, I can't stress enough that it is imperative that you *do* something with the new information that you learn from this book to make a positive change in your life.

Let's be clear. You must learn to recognize when PCT is monopolizing your attention. Not being able to recognize PCT is like sleepwalking around a pool when you can't swim—it's awfully hard to protect yourself from what you can't see.

At the end of each chapter, we point out the three most important takeaways that we want to make sure you *know*, and we identify one thing we want you to *do*. Don't skip or blow this part off. There is critical information in the "Do" sections that is fundamental to adopting and maintaining RSF. I know you will be tempted to move right on to the next chapter and think, "I'll do it later." "I'll do it later" is the language of a loser. That may sound harsh, but it is simply another way of saying, "It's not important enough to do right now," which means it's probably not going to get done. Do not allow yourself to say, "I'll do it later."

"I'll do it later" is the language of a loser.

Remember, knowing something does nothing to change your life; *doing* something does. We are not writing this book to waste your time. We won't be asking you to do trust falls or any other goofy exercises. Everything we ask you to do requires very little time but produces significant returns toward adopting an RSF mindset. We guarantee you will like the results of developing the RSF mindset. Please invest a little time into doing the work to make it happen. Putting some effort into yourself is far better than not putting any effort in because you are afraid of not being perfect. In many instances, *done is better than perfect,* and in the "1 Thing to *Do*" sections of this book, that is certainly the case.

③ THINGS TO *KNOW*

1. Problem-centric thought (PCT) is biologically wired into all of us. We have an intrinsic inclination toward focusing on problems. It exists within us as individuals, and it also exists within society.
2. If you are the type of person who often focuses on problems and negativity, you are not broken. You are typical. However, allowing yourself to be typical will eventually lead to a significant breakdown in your health, happiness, and success.
3. The first step toward combating PCT is to learn to recognize it. The human mind can only fully focus on one thing at a time. If you are focused on the problem, you cannot be focused on what you are going to do about it.

① THING TO *DO*

We are so good at being problem-focused, that we often don't even realize that we are doing it. Combat PCT by starting to *recognize* the times when you allow yourself to focus on problems.

The See PCT Challenge

Take one minute to work on recognizing PCT. For the next minute, count how many negative thoughts you have. Each time you recognize that you were thinking about a problem or something negative, give yourself a point. Tally your points after the one-minute period. Whatever your score is, multiply it by 60 to calculate how many times per hour PCT invades your mind. Then multiply that number by 16 (assuming you sleep for 8 of the 24 hours in a day). That is how many times per day PCT invades your mind.

Just so you know, the average number of times a person doing this challenge has a PCT-related thought is five. That's 4,800 negative thoughts daily! But that's also the number of times daily you have the opportunity to improve your life.

If you really want to blow your mind, complete the same exercise while listening to others conversing or while watching a news program. I warn you in advance: Accepting this challenge will cause you to become much more sensitive to the negativity of others around you. Please don't take this challenge as your responsibility to stop other people from being negative. Recognizing PCT in others can help you become more sensitive to how PCT invades your life. This is an exercise of recognition; we want you to become more aware of just how natural PCT is. Later, you will learn how to attack and defeat it, but for now, it's all about improving your ability to spot it.

2

Expectancy Theory

That Which You
Focus on Expands

When I was going through graduate school, part of my training was in relationship counseling. In any relationship counseling program in the country, the textbooks are still teaching the technique called the "ABCs of communication": A = "I feel," B = "when you," and C = "in this situation."

Shortly after I finished graduate school, my first couple came to see me in my office. They were two physicians living in St. Louis. They'd been married for 30 years, but living in separate bedrooms for the past 10 years. When I learned that fact, I thought to myself, "That's all right. I've got the ABCs of communication, and I'm going to have them back on track in no time."

In the first session I laid the ABCs of communication on them, and I sat back and watched it go. And go it did . . . right into World War III. "I feel . . . when you . . ." quickly turned into versions of "You always," or "You never," and then into complete frustration and anger. They were both wishing they had stuck to their separate bedrooms rather than venturing into my office. It didn't take me long to figure out that if a couple comes into my office with a certain number of problems, and they leave with *more* problems, they would probably stop coming in for counseling sooner rather than later.

After that first session, I remember thinking, "What in the heck just happened?"

When I thought about what I was really doing with the ABCs of communication, I realized I was basically inviting people to talk about their problems. More than that, I was asking them to *really* dig into those problems. And they were leaving much more miserable than when they had arrived. I needed to figure this one out quickly, or else I wouldn't have a practice for long.

For the second session, I changed my approach and asked each of them to identify one thing about themselves that they wanted to work on improving for the sake of the relationship. The husband determined that he wanted to work on giving his wife more compliments, and the wife determined that she wanted to be more present when she returned home from work during the week. This became *much* more of a productive start to our work together.

Session after session, they committed to spending their time searching for solutions and figuring out how to implement the positive change. I established the "10-minute rule," which held that after the first 10 minutes of any meeting, no one was allowed to talk about problems, and the focus had to shift to what could be done to make the situation better. After 18 months of therapy, the couple decided to successfully terminate counseling, as their relationship had improved dramatically. Over the years, the couple would come in for tune-ups every now and again, and they even brought their children in to learn the solution-focused mindset. To this day, the couple remains married, and I still use the 10-minute rule in all of my marriage counseling sessions.

THE GREAT MYTH

We're all familiar with the idea that "talking about our problems will lead us to solutions." What I witnessed that first day in my office didn't support that idea, not by a long shot. I went on a search for empirical evidence and guess what I found?

Zip.

There is no empirical evidence *anywhere* that supports that idea. In fact, it's quite the opposite. The idea that talking about or thinking about your problems leads you to solutions is what I call the "Great Myth." You hear about it all the time, and you may have even experienced it in a therapist's office, but in the research and in my experience, it flat out does not work. Most people who start talking about their problems get sucked into the PCT tornado and can't find their way out. The more we focus on our problems, the more problems we have. The World War III–level fight I witnessed with the married couple in my office that day started with the best of intentions to improve their relationship, but continued to take one wrong turn after another.

The more we focus on our problems,
the more problems we have.

Have you ever bought a new car and suddenly noticed that same make and model all over the place? The focus on your specific car type immediately opens your eyes to it everywhere you look. This is the same principle I witnessed in action in my office with the married physicians. When your focus is on something, whether it's a shiny new car or a behavior that annoys you about your partner, you start to notice more and more of those same things. We already know we are inclined to focus on problems (PCT), and this can be a recipe for disaster unless we learn to combat it.

WHAT IS EXPECTANCY THEORY?

Expectancy theory is the basis of much of performance psychology and its practices, and it's certainly the basis of all of the fundamentals Ellen and I teach our clients. The definition of expectancy theory is *that which you focus on expands*. We know that what we think causes us to feel and behave in certain ways. If we can learn to control our thoughts, we can control our feelings and our behavior.

> **Expectancy theory:** that which you focus on expands

Not only are you going to learn how to combat PCT, you are going to learn how to wage war against it and completely destroy it. By understanding PCT and expectancy theory, you learn two of the most important pieces of fundamental knowledge for arming yourself against mental weakness.

If we can learn to control our thoughts, we can control our feelings and our behavior.

The more we focus on problems, the more problems we will create. It's really that simple. Although simple in concept, breaking free from the damage that PCT combined with expectancy theory can do requires mental toughness. It requires Relentless Solution Focus (RSF), which we will begin to talk about in the next chapter. The good news is that as much damage as we can do by focusing on problems, just as much positive change can occur by maintaining a focus on solutions. *Expectancy theory works every bit as well with the positive as it does with the negative.* This book will teach you how to develop and maintain that focus, but first, it is important to understand how damaging our typical train of thought can be.

Let's go back to what we talked about earlier. Remember that it's quite typical to do 99 things right throughout the day and one thing less than perfectly, and have your mind focus on that one imperfection. Let's say you're driving home from work, and you are beating yourself up about the mistake. You begin feeling less and less positive about life. By the time you get home, you have put yourself in a pretty sour mood. You walk into the house, and immediately, you are met with a problem from your spouse that came up while you were at work. Because you are already in a foul mood, you respond in a less than ideal manner, and now you have started an argument. Then you get into a yelling match with one of your children, and you ground him for life. The next thing you know, you are waking up the next morning on the couch with a sore back. That which you focus on *expands*.

Now, if I were in your shoes, I would probably be thinking to myself, "OK, I see how focusing on problems causes more problems. No need to read any further. I have this figured out. Moving forward, I am going to just tell myself not to think about problems." If only it were that easy. Remember, PCT is biologically ingrained. Your brain is built to focus on problems, and it's almost impossible to stop without the proper training.

Try this experiment. Tell yourself, "Don't think about a pink elephant wearing blue running shoes," and for 15 seconds, try not to think about that pink elephant with blue running shoes. My guess is that even though you told yourself not to think about that elephant, that is exactly what you did think about. This is known as the *theory of dominant thought*. We move toward, take action on, and form memories around the thoughts that are dominant in our mind. Telling yourself not to think about something keeps that subject as a dominant thought in your mind. The dominant thought is the elephant, and that is precisely the issue we have with PCT. *Problems* are the dominant and natural thought. To stop PCT, we must use something known as *thought replacement*. To stop thinking about the pink elephant, you must simply force yourself to picture something else. For example, focus on a bright red hot-air balloon instead.

The same technique is true for PCT. To stop thinking about problems, we must learn to identify and focus on the solution. Try the experiment again, but this time, for 15 seconds, anytime the elephant begins to enter your mind, replace it with the bright red hot-air balloon. Remember, your brain can fully focus on only one thing at a time. If you are focused on a bright red hot-air balloon, it becomes easier *not* to think about that pink elephant wearing blue running shoes. In the same way, if you are focused on a solution, you cannot also be focused on the problem.

If you just took the time to do that thought replacement exercise, well done. That was your first exercise in thought control. If you could do that, then you can eventually learn to train your mind to replace *all* problems with solutions.

> **Theory of dominant thought:** We move toward, take action on, and form memories around the thoughts that are dominant in our mind.
>
> **Thought replacement:** The mind can fully focus on only one thing at a time. To get rid of a thought, replace it with another.

Early in my career, I often worked with young athletes who had the talent and aspirations to reach high levels of performance. Parents would bring their children to me to help them gain the mental edge to reach the next level of success. Many times, it was the parents who would gain as much, if not more, insight into how their own mentality was affecting and influencing their children. Matthew came in one afternoon with his mother, Sandy. Matthew was a successful high school golfer, who had won several national-level tournaments over the past few years, but he was struggling to maintain consistency. When I asked Matthew what he hoped to improve about his performance as a golfer, Sandy was the first to speak. She jumped in and said, "Matthew plays great in practices, but lately he seems to choke under the pressure of tournaments." She proceeded to give me three separate examples of tournaments where he hadn't performed to his potential. "His coaches all say the same thing," she continued. "He just seems to be getting less and less consistent."

Matthew had been hearing over and over from his parents, his coaches, and his own self-talk that he was an inconsistent golfer. Other people can be really good at pointing out our problems, even though we do a good enough job of it ourselves. He was going into every tournament expecting to blow it somehow, and he would find a way to do just that. Like a self-fulfilling prophecy, what you believe, you make happen.

What started with a few bad putts turned into a few bad holes and eventually a few bad tournaments. Before he knew it, Matthew's confidence had tanked. The more he thought about how poorly he was playing, the more poorly he played. While Matthew needed some tools to help him maintain his focus on the control points for his success on the course, he also needed to become aware of how his negative self-talk was affecting his game. When Matthew learned to start controlling what he allowed to stay in his mind, he gained more control over his performance. Whenever he caught himself thinking debilitating thoughts such as, "I have to make this shot!" or "Don't blow this," or "I choke under pressure," he quickly replaced those thoughts with more positive ones like, "See the target, soft hands, follow through," or "I am at my best when it matters most."

He forced himself to think of positive performance cues that increased his focus on what he needed to do to be successful. He also began to identify what he did well after each tournament, no matter how badly he felt that he had played. Matthew worked on being relentless with his thought control. At first, he was inconsistent, catching himself being negative, but then quickly shifting his thoughts to his performance cues. Other times, his normal negative thinking would happen without him even being aware. But over time, Mathew began to recognize the negative thoughts more quickly and more often, and his ability to shift to the positive eventually became much more consistent. Just as PCT had taken down his confidence, his new focus on his control points for success and what he was doing *well* on the course started to expand. A few successes in small tournaments turned into a few successes in bigger tournaments. Matthew eventually received a full-ride athletic scholarship to a Division I university, and now he is positioning himself for a promising professional career on the golf course.

I also challenged Matthew's mother, Sandy, to recognize at least two things Matthew did well during every tournament. She was to spend the first two minutes of every car ride home after tournaments talking to Matthew about his "done-wells" and expressing what made her proud of him. After two minutes, she could bring up anything else about his performance she wanted, but she had to devote those first two minutes to the positive. Sandy found that she often didn't even feel the need to move to something negative or critical because she could tell that Matthew was excited and motivated about continuing to improve what they discussed during those two minutes. She also reported that she started applying this rule to her own evaluations of her workday performance. She forced herself to devote the first two minutes of her car ride home from work each day to thinking about what she did well or what she enjoyed about work that day. Not only did her performance at work improve significantly, she also discovered that she was becoming more excited to go to work each day after making this one simple change.

This is a good time to ask a very important question: *How do you nourish your own self-confidence?* This question is important enough to spend the next 20 seconds thinking about your answer. Be honest with yourself. How do you nourish your self-confidence?

When asked this question, most people don't really have an answer. If you didn't have an answer, don't worry. By the time you finish this book, you will know why it's important and exactly how to do so.

Remember the "See PCT Challenge" from Chapter 1? That is a great exercise because it is helpful in recognizing first, our PCT tendency, and second, how expectancy theory plays a part in our thoughts. It is common to start thinking about problems, which then leads to even more thoughts about problems. Expectancy theory can work just as well *for* you as it can work *against* you. Our guess is that the "See PCT Challenge" also forced you to notice how often *other* people complain. It is usually much easier to recognize negative behaviors in other people than it is in ourselves. As much as you may be thinking that your coworkers wasted so much time complaining during your morning meeting, if given the same challenge, they may likely be thinking the same about you.

One of the most influential people in my life is the legendary Coach John Wooden. The day I had the good fortune of meeting Coach Wooden is one I will never forget. Coach was in his 90s, and I had the opportunity to accompany my good friends Andy Hill and Tom Bartow to Coach Wooden's condo. His home was filled with photos of him standing with the greatest of the greats, as well as photos of his own family and loved ones. It was evident from the photos that Coach Wooden had influenced countless others as he did me. This is a man who knew and lived by the secrets to success, and I wanted in.

A lesson that I take from Coach Wooden is one that he actually learned from his father at a young age: the "two sets of three."

Never lie, never cheat, never steal; don't whine, don't complain, don't make excuses. Most of us probably engage in whining and complaining more than we like to think, but Coach Wooden and his father knew the importance of being abnormal in this way.

The extremely successful are not standing around complaining about their problems because they have learned the inefficiency of doing so. Statements as seemingly innocent as, "I'm so tired," or "I am dreading going to this meeting," or "I can't believe my boss said that to me," are affecting your productivity, energy, and focus more than you think. Complaining about an issue cannot help but cause your mind to magnify the issue. Suddenly, you feel much more tired than you really are because you have been reminding yourself of it all day, or you begin to dread that afternoon meeting so much that you cannot focus on your morning work. Many times, people find that by simply *not* complaining about an issue and moving on from it, the issue seems to dissipate sooner than one might expect. In the meantime, you haven't ruined the rest of your day by devoting more attention to the negative.

People initiate coaching with us for many different reasons. Some have hit a slump and want help coming out of it, some are already on a roll and want to take advantage of that momentum, and some have a personal issue holding them back. Albert was a client of Ellen's who initially came to her because of a "nemesis" he had within his company. Let's call him Randy. Albert found himself consumed with frustration and anger with Randy because he felt that Randy was holding back his advancement within the company and just "had it out" for him. It was unclear what caused Randy's apparent contempt for Albert, but over the course of the past seven years, Albert was very aware that Randy disliked him. There was never a big blowout or incident, but Albert often complained about getting a negative "vibe" from Randy. "He ignores me every time we are at an event together, and he is short and cold every time we do have an interaction. I try to make an effort with him, but it never seems to make a difference." Albert understood the importance of addressing his issues with Randy because, frankly, it was making him miserable at work, and he said his wife was tired of hearing him complain about it.

Randy did not work in the same building as Albert, so they rarely crossed paths throughout the week, but that didn't stop Albert from obsessing over him. Albert had access to everyone in the company's numbers, and he found himself checking Randy's production several times per day. Ellen quickly learned that Albert was basically an expert on Randy's performance. When Randy was having a good week, it would ruin the rest of Albert's day. When Randy was having a down week, Albert would feel good for about 30 seconds, but then continue to check his numbers incessantly for the rest of the day to make sure they were still poor.

Albert's obsession with Randy had quite simply become its own animal. The more he checked Randy's numbers, the more he thought about Randy. The more he thought about Randy, the bigger part of his life Randy became. The bigger part of his life Randy became, the more of an impact Randy had on him. *That which you focus on expands.*

Every second Albert was thinking about Randy was a second he *wasn't* thinking about his own performance. He wasn't performing badly, by any means. In fact, Albert's production was consistently higher than Randy's. Their numbers were close, but Albert was outperforming him. Albert's nemesis, though, still consumed a lot of energy that could otherwise be spent on what was actually important to him, like improving his job performance or enjoying his family.

By this point, you may be thinking that Albert's obsession might make him a good candidate for a Lifetime movie of the week, but his story is actually quite common. Most of us probably have a "Randy" in our lives—someone or something that consumes much more of our focus than we would like. In fact, we might be embarrassed to admit just how much focus we place on that someone or something. Albert *is* unique, however, because he recognized this in himself and wanted to improve.

The first thing that Ellen did was give Albert one rule: he was not allowed to check Randy's production. This simple act that took him only a few clicks of the mouse had become so much of a habit that he did it almost without thinking. Even though checking Randy's numbers took only about two minutes out of Albert's schedule each day, the impact that it had extended well beyond those two minutes. While it sounds simple, this was not an easy task. Sometimes Albert would find himself halfway through the mouse clicks to get to Randy's numbers before even realizing what he was doing. Eventually, he became better at stopping himself sooner. He even stuck a note to his computer that read, "Stay Focused!" While he wasn't perfect, he cut down on how often he would check the numbers from several times a day to about once per week.

The less time he was allowing himself to spend thinking about Randy's performance, the better he felt at work and the more positive energy he had to put toward his own prospects and clients. It is not a coincidence that Albert's production increased by 30 percent in the next 11 months by making this one simple adjustment. The real win for Albert, however, was that he became much happier at work (and at home) by not allowing his focus to expand in a negative direction. He was able to actually enjoy the success he was experiencing.

Of course, there are issues that do not just go away by not allowing yourself to complain about them or focus on them. No matter how much you don't allow yourself to complain about the market, your revenue is not going to magically increase on its own. For these situations, not allowing yourself to complain about how bad you have it forces you to come up with a solution to the problem sooner. Think about it, every minute you are spending complaining about the market is a minute you are not spending thinking about ways to hit your numbers for the month. The same mechanism that makes it normal for us to want to engage in complaining kicks in to make us come up with a solution. Our brain does everything in its power to get rid of those negative feelings. If complaining them away is not an option, guess what—you actually have to *do* something about them.

Most people mistakenly believe that if they can figure out who is to blame or what the underlying reason or fault for the problem is, then the solution will magically appear. As common as this logic is, unfortunately, it is quite ineffective. The truth is, this approach of "finding the reason" pales in comparison to realizing the actual cause of the problem is oftentimes irrelevant when compared to becoming relentless about finding that first step forward. Translation: Quit worrying about who is to blame and why it happened in the first place, and start thinking, "Who cares who or what is to blame? I just want to move forward, and the first thing I can do to make that happen is. . . ."

You may still be thinking, "Well, before I begin coming up with solutions, I need to fully understand the problem." If you are disciplined enough to focus on problems for short periods (less than 60 seconds) and then always get to the solutions, that's great. But very few people have such discipline. Most people who start talking about problems get stuck in the problem focus, and they don't ever get to the solution side of things. When you compare focusing on understanding the problem completely versus putting your energy into understanding the solution, there is no contest. The rule on understanding the problem is simple: Do not allow yourself more than 60 seconds to do so before forcing your thoughts to solutions. Following the 60-second rule should give you ample time to figure out what you are dealing with.

EXPECTANCY THEORY
AND CONFIDENCE

The power of expectancy theory cannot be overstated largely because of the role it plays in confidence. Research confirms that confidence is the number one variable affecting a person's performance. This isn't rocket science. If a person allows his mind to focus on his shortcomings, confidence is naturally low. If he can get himself more focused on what he is doing well, confidence improves, thus leading to increased ability and potential for other tasks and activities. Focusing on problems decreases confidence, whereas a focus on solutions greatly enhances it. People with high confidence are much more coachable, and they make improvements much more efficiently.

Confidence is the number one variable affecting a person's performance. Focusing on problems decreases confidence, whereas a focus on solutions greatly enhances it.

I worked with the leader of a team of about 10 associates in a major finance company several years back. He sought out my help because he was struggling to find ways to motivate his team. His team was responsible for bringing in a great deal of revenue for the firm, so not performing well was not an option. During a leadership review process that human resources conducted with his team, he received complaints that his associates did not feel like he recognized and rewarded their efforts and contributions. He was frustrated with this feedback, especially because he felt that most members of his team were falling short of expectations.

I asked him how often he recognized what the individuals on his team were doing well, and he responded, "I always give them positive feedback whenever they do something well. Lately, the problem is that they don't often do what I need them to do." He went on to say, "If they were performing better, I would recognize it."

My client was reacting like any typical, rational human by expecting his team to actually do great work if they wanted to be recognized for it. His team felt they should be recognized more, while he felt they should be doing more to earn the recognition. The reality is that both sides were probably correct. Being correct in this situation, unfortunately, did nothing for the productivity of the team.

I encouraged him to start making a conscious effort to recognize at least one done-well for a member of his team every day. Instead of waiting for something to stand out to him, he would need to put in the effort to look for it to reach his daily quota. At first, he was reluctant. He said, "Why would I recognize them for falling short of expectations? I don't want to celebrate mediocrity." I instructed him that a done-well is *not* like a participation award. Participation awards go out to everyone, whether they deserve credit or not. The key is to actually find something they are doing well, something worthy of recognition. Don't invent something positive that doesn't exist. Instead, *search* for those positive actions that are present, and comment on those.

After only two weeks of following the done-well plan, his second-in-command pulled him aside and told him that the team was aware of his efforts and that it was making a big difference with morale. In particular, one of the team members actually gathered the team together and said it was obvious that the boss cared about the team and the project, and that it was their responsibility to pick up the pace. Eventually, they began doing more things that he actually found worthy of recognizing. It became easier for him to find things to celebrate. Recognizing the done-wells created a positive cycle of performance.

It is not common to have a constant radar for what is working well because PCT naturally sets your radar to what is not working well. A focus on what people are doing well, remember, results in people doing even more things well. This is a snowball effect that great leaders absolutely use to their advantage.

Let's be clear. This is not an excuse to be soft or to overlook needed improvements. The simple rule to follow when evaluating performance is *always begin with the positive.* When you start by recognizing those done-wells first, the stage is set for a strong foundation of confidence, and this increases open-mindedness and motivation for improvement. Starting with the positive actually gives individuals and teams the inner strength to better execute the needed improvements.

With evaluation, always begin with the positive.

Think about the great football coach Bill Belichick, who is widely considered to be one of the greatest coaches in NFL history. Many people know how demanding he is of his players and staff; however, few are aware how he can push those around him so hard without breeding resentment. Coach Belichick knows that the only way to win consistently at the highest level is to be as good at recognizing what is being done well as what needs to be improved. It is not uncommon for Belichick to ask his players what was wrong after a seemingly great play. A lineman had recorded a sack or a receiver had made a terrific catch. The problem? The other teammates had not congratulated or recognized their teammate's contribution in any way. Not recognizing positive behavior is as counterproductive to success as not having an obsession for improvement.

If your boss is constantly pointing out your shortcomings and is frustrated with you for not performing well, would that motivate you to perform better? Probably not. You would probably come up with a reason your boss is wrong or rude or unfair, and your confidence would take quite a beating. *That which you focus on expands.* My client was focused on what his team was doing poorly, and that resulted in more sub-par performance. When someone points out what you are doing well, that increases your confidence and motivation, which results in you having the motivation and ability to do more things well.

Allowing yourself to focus on the negative—those things that aren't going well or the bad in the world—makes a major negative impact on your overall level of health and happiness. Anyone who has let a small worry snowball into a sea of anxiety can relate to this. If you have ever looked up a small health symptom on Google and an hour later found yourself still scrolling, convinced you have a rare, life-threatening disease, you have experienced this. Everything from the television shows you watch, the social influencers you follow on Instagram, and the news outlets you read plays on expectancy theory to influence your thoughts, beliefs, and behaviors. Think about it like this: your brain is like a sponge, and having a focus on negativity and imperfections is like soaking that sponge in dirty, disgusting water. However, if you can learn to change your focus to the things you are doing well and the positives in the world, it is like putting fresh spring water in that sponge. What type of water are you letting soak into your sponge on a daily basis?

③ THINGS TO *KNOW*

1. Expectancy theory: that which you focus on *expands*.
2. PCT is so damaging because of how it intersects with expectancy theory. Thinking about and focusing on problems is our normal course of thought. Unfortunately, this compounds and creates more problems.
3. Expectancy theory works every bit as well with the positive as it does with the negative. If we can learn to focus on what is going well or what is working, we will have more positive performances and increased confidence.

① THING TO *DO*

For the next three days, set a reminder on your phone or on your calendar to recognize one done-well in another person each day. Choose someone in your life (coworker, spouse, child, friend) and point out something he or she did well. Remember, this is not a participation trophy. Make sure the positive recognition is genuine. It could be as simple as, "You do a great job of answering my emails quickly," or "I love the effort you put into connecting with our children at bedtime," or "I saw how aggressive you were at getting back on defense during practice tonight." You may find that you have to work a little harder to recognize something positive that someone else is doing and that the shortcomings come to mind first. You may also find that the people receiving the compliments attempt to downplay or deflect it. Compliments are rare and at times surprising because PCT is ingrained in all of us. You may have to put effort into coming up with a done-well each day, and that is a good sign that you need to be doing this exercise. Starting to recognize the positives about other people is a good start to learning how to recognize your own daily done-wells. This is another fundamental exercise in thought control. Doing this regularly (or at least for the next three days) teaches you how to be more conscious of your thinking and grows your ability for effective thought replacement.

3

Relentless Solution Focus

There Is Always a Solution—*Always*

n the fall of 2011, a 31-year-old Rick Scheeler sat in a somewhat uncomfortable chair that minutes earlier had been dragged into the oversized conference room of his Rockwood, Ohio, office where I was conducting a coaching class. Rick had been working as a financial planner for a number of years and was very unhappy. He was working 80 hours per week and feeling like there had to be more to life. Rick's typical day had him arriving at the office at 6:30 a.m. and staying most nights until 9:00 or 10:00 p.m. Rick enjoyed the work; the problem was he was just doing way too much of it. Even if he did have time to spend with his family, he was too exhausted to enjoy it. He was discouraged and ready to leave the business and pursue something else.

Rick decided in early 2011 that he would hire a business coach to try to make things better for himself and his family.

His managing partner suggested that he consider working with me for a year. I was already scheduled to conduct this coaching class with a number of Rick's colleagues in Ohio, and although he wasn't overly optimistic that I could help, he decided he would hire me for one year to see if I could do anything for him. Day in and day out Rick was becoming more and more focused on problems with no framework for dealing with adversity. Hiring me as a coach was his last-ditch effort to figure out if he could make his career as a financial advisor work.

When I first met Rick, it was obvious that he was in a bad place. As I passionately introduced my coaching platform to the 25 or so advisors in the room that morning, I could see a distant look in his eyes and a sadness across his face.

The first thing I went to work on with Rick was getting him to understand that there is *always* a solution. There is *always* something that can be done to improve the situation, and if he would become relentless about searching for and finding those solutions, he would immediately experience some relief from the pain he was feeling. Human beings have a built-in, DNA-level need for safety, security, and control. When we don't experience these, we feel hopeless, depressed, and sometimes angry. The key to moving forward in life is to develop the ability to feel in control. No matter the situation, there is always something we can do to improve. We have control if we *choose* to have control.

Rick's first priority was to figure out how to better control his schedule. He just simply could not keep working 80 hours a week. When we first talked about working less, his response was, "Jason, I can't afford to work less. My family needs this income." I gently reminded him, "Rick, there is *always* a solution. *Always*. We just need to open our minds and find it." At the time, Rick was making $280,000 a year. As much as that is, for a family with six children, a mortgage, and college loans to pay off, money was tight. Reducing his income did not seem to be a viable solution for Rick. We needed to figure out how he could make more money while working fewer hours. Again, I reminded Rick (and myself) of a very valuable principle I learned a number of years earlier: "There is *always* a solution. *Always.*"

Imagine the look on Rick's face when he heard my first question: "Rick, how can you work 79 hours weekly and still make at least what you made last year?" After realizing that I was serious, his solution-focus wheels began to spin. After some thought, he responded. "Actually, I think the first step is to set some boundaries for myself and my hours. I think if I set an end time—a time I must leave by—I will just find a way to get the work done."

Even though I asked Rick for only a one-hour reduction in his weekly hours, he started by setting a start time of 7:00 a.m. and an end time of 7:00 p.m. Monday through Friday, and he allowed himself to work only five hours on Saturday. His new schedule was a 15-hour improvement. For three months, we watched closely to make sure that the new hours wouldn't have a negative impact on his income. Rick was correct. He wasn't seeing any decrease whatsoever in his income, and he was finding a way to get the same amount of work done in significantly fewer hours.

Working less was allowing Rick to show up for work with more energy, and he was feeling better about himself and his life. This slowly started to have a positive impact on his enjoyment level and desire to get to work. Rick began to realize that he had forgotten how much he actually enjoyed helping people improve their financial situation and how good he was at doing it. Twelve months later, Rick was working approximately 65 hours weekly, his income had risen to over $350,000 annually, and most important, he was significantly happier. Rick made a point to tell me that his happiness wasn't tied to the money, but rather to feeling so much more in control of his life. He had more time to spend with his family, and he could put more energy into being a great husband and father.

Although Rick still wasn't satisfied with where his life was, he admitted there was major improvement and that it all began when he opened his mind to the idea that "there is *always* a solution. *Always.*" Rick commented, "I had never considered that even a one-hour improvement was a solution. I would either not even think about solutions because I was so wrapped up in the problem, or if I *did* think about solutions, I would focus on how to solve the problem in its entirety. I was literally looking for perfection. I couldn't figure out how to go from 80 hours per week to 40 hours per week. It seemed hopeless, so I had literally stopped trying."

Rick and I continued to work together for another six years. He continued to reduce how many hours he worked weekly while posting consistent gains in his personal happiness, health, and professional success. He was working a very manageable 50 hours weekly, and he was making four times what he had been earning just a few years earlier. He was exercising on a daily basis, and most important, he was feeling proud of himself as a husband and father. Then the unthinkable happened.

On September 25, 2018, Rick kissed his children and wife good-bye before heading to the airport for a business trip to New York. After a couple of days of work in New York City, Rick was glad to be heading back home to Ohio. He was scheduled to arrive home early enough to spend some time with his family before going to bed. Unfortunately, his plane was delayed, and he didn't arrive home until after 2:00 a.m. Rick woke the next morning at 6:00 a.m., quietly dressed, and left the house before anyone else was awake so he could be on time for a 7:00 a.m. client meeting.

The morning of September 27 was a fairly typical morning at the Scheeler house. The children all woke and got themselves ready for school with help from their mom, Ellie. The second oldest child, Mary, who was a senior in high school, was her normal bubbly self. Mary was a special child. She was born with Down syndrome, but that isn't what made her so special. Mary was full of love and happiness. Her smile was infectious, and she used it all the time. She was everyone's sunshine, even on rainy days.

Mary loved basketball, and on this particular morning, even though it was early and a school day, she was already thinking about getting home from school and shooting baskets in the family's driveway. Mary was one of those children to whom other children were drawn. Many of her best friends were on the basketball team. In 2015, Mary had been asked to serve as assistant basketball coach for the Mason Jr. basketball team. She wore her "Assistant Coach" embroidered team jacket with pride everywhere she went.

After school the day of September 27, 2018, Mary had stopped on her bike at the neighborhood mini-mart for a snack before going home to shoot some hoops. Upon leaving the mini-mart that day, Mary inadvertently swayed her bike into traffic and was hit by an oncoming car. She was immediately taken to the hospital, but unfortunately, she never recovered. Mary Scheeler passed away from internal injuries on September 28, 2018.

As any parent can imagine, Rick and Ellie Scheeler were crushed. Rick forced himself to remember the words, "There is *always* a solution. *Always.*" The only thought on Rick's mind was, "My sweet Mary is gone. How can there be a solution to this?"

Rick and I spoke on September 29. He said to me, "What's odd about this is that I really don't feel anything. It's like my brain can't or won't accept the reality. All of our friends and family have been so great, so supportive. I see the pain that everyone else is experiencing, and I just can't get myself to feel anything. I feel nothing. I'm numb."

Rick initially focused his attention on helping his family find solutions. He knew the most positive mindset in the world couldn't change what had happened. Now he needed to focus on how his family would deal with the tragedy, how they would move forward with their lives. Rick's solution was to remember Mary—to honor her by keeping her beautiful spirit alive in each of her family members. He was diligent in teaching his family that "There is always a solution. Always." Rick didn't take responsibility for finding each person's solution; however, he was relentless about asking them solution-focused questions that would force them to look inside themselves and find something to help them get through each day.

When he would see a particular family member struggling, he would ask, "What is one thing you can do right now to make this better?" Sometimes the answer was, "Cry. Give myself permission to grieve and cry." Other times the answer was to tell stories of Mary, to think of her smile, or to play a family game of basketball. The Scheeler house focused on solutions, and slowly, ever so slowly, they began to heal.

"What is one thing you can do right now to make this better?"

Eventually, Rick's numbness was replaced with pain. There were times when he felt strong and other times when the loss was seemingly unbearable. I gently reminded Rick of three things:

1. There is *always* a solution. *Always.*
2. It is important to focus on what you do have instead of what you do not have, even when it is really hard to do so.
3. In tough times, it is essential to fight the urge to focus on what isn't going well, but rather to be relentless about recognizing what you are doing well.

Rick worked to control his thoughts. In tough times, he forced himself to think about his remaining children and loving wife. He made himself feel and give love to his family and friends, and he spent time daily writing down on paper three things he did well that day.

On October 25, one month after Mary's passing, Rick sent me the following note:

> Jason, my daughter had a tough day at volleyball last week. She was working so hard at it and made some silly early mistakes, and she had a bit of a breakdown. When we got home, I had her read your chapter on RSF and how to talk to yourself. She took notes and wrote in her journal. She shared what she learned with her team. Today in a tournament, she made a couple early mistakes again, but stayed strong and had a great game, as did the rest of the team. They won and placed third in their conference.
>
> My brother has hit rock bottom in life. He has asked me for help with his kids. I told him I would consider, but as a precondition, I wanted him to read a few of my notes on RSF. He promised he would. Once he starts recognizing what he has done well and what to improve, he will be a different man.
>
> Your impact is generational. Thank you, my friend.

Rick and his family continue to make progress. As each month passes, they heal a bit more. As part of the healing process, the family set a goal to raise $100,000 in Mary's honor to be donated to her favorite charity for playgrounds for children with special needs. In the first three months, they raised more than $250,000 in Mary's honor.

WHAT IS RELENTLESS SOLUTION FOCUS?

Relentless Solution Focus (RSF) is simply defined as *within 60 seconds, replacing all negative thoughts with solution-focused thinking.* Although simple in definition, at times this can be extremely difficult to do. RSF is mental toughness. They are one and the same. No one needs mental toughness when he is winning the game by four touchdowns or when life is going uncharacteristically well. It's in those times when you are losing by three runs in the bottom of the ninth or when life is beating you up that you really need the strength between your ears. Think about it for a moment, when was the last time you were *relentless* about anything? If you are struggling to come up with an answer, trust me, you are not alone. Most people these days are so overwhelmed by trying to get everything checked off their to-do lists or living up to other people's expectations that being relentless doesn't even cross their minds. I want you to know that just because being relentless is rare doesn't mean you can't learn to do it. In fact, I will tell you that it is *essential* for you to learn to be relentless. There will be times when you don't want to believe that there is a solution to a problem you are facing. Being relentless means that you know there is *always* a solution. *Always*. You deserve it, and you can do it, and this book is going to show you exactly how to do it.

> **Relentless Solution Focus:** within 60 seconds, replacing all negative thoughts with solution-focused thinking

Let's be clear, mental toughness is not easy. It is not supposed to be easy, but it can be learned. You can learn how to fight through life's most difficult challenges and all the negative thinking that goes along with it by being relentless about focusing on solutions. You can learn to more effectively work through every single problem life throws at you and to attack and defeat all of that self-imposed negativity. That is precisely what RSF will do for you. Recognizing the fundamental differences between mental weakness (PCT) and mental toughness (RSF) will make it much easier to begin developing the foundation for having RSF.

Mental toughness is not easy. It is not supposed to be easy, but it can be learned.

Optimism and the Science of RSF

Individuals with the RSF mindset are scientifically proven to experience a significant increase in health, happiness, and success. Internalizing the RSF mindset decreases the likelihood of cancer (by 16 percent), heart disease (by 38 percent), stroke (by 39 percent), and respiratory disease (by 38 percent). Replacing problem-centric thought with potential solutions will make you happier, you will make friends faster, your friendships will be more lasting, you will sleep better, and you will experience significantly more success than your peers who choose not to adopt the RSF mindset. In terms of the key to success and well-being, it is hard to argue that there is anything more important than developing an RSF mindset.

Individuals with the RSF mindset are scientifically proven to experience a significant increase in health, happiness, and success.

RSF is a guaranteed winner, and it's scientifically proven. To better understand the science behind RSF, it is important to recognize the link between RSF and optimism. Think of RSF as a concrete way to define and measure optimism. Optimism, as a construct, has been extensively researched. Dr. Martin Seligman, known as the father of the positive psychology movement, studied optimism for more than 25 years. In discussing the difference between pessimists and optimists, Seligman writes:

> The defining characteristic of pessimists is that they tend to believe bad events will last a long time, will undermine everything they do, and are their own fault. The optimists, who are confronted with the same hard knocks of this world, think about misfortune in the opposite way. They tend to believe defeat is just a temporary setback. . . . Such

people are unfazed by defeat. Confronted by a bad situation, they perceive it as a challenge and try harder.

Having an RSF mindset is essentially another way of stating that a person has high levels of optimism. While optimism has been widely researched and the benefits are unmistakable, this is the first book of its kind that actually teaches people exactly *how* to be more optimistic. You are about to learn the proven step-by-step process of training yourself to develop RSF and to become more optimistic along the way. And the best news of all is that with training, anyone can become *relentless* about choosing solution-focused thought.

The real benefit of RSF is that it serves as a concrete way of replacing PCT. Replacing is integral. You already know that it is not good to think about or focus on problems, and we've already established that you can't just tell yourself *not* to think about your problems or the negatives in your life. That doesn't work.

Remember the pink elephant example from Chapter 2? Telling yourself *not* to think about or focus on something is a waste of breath, and it actually makes it much more likely that you *will* focus on it. The only true way of not thinking about that pink elephant is, instead, to shift your thinking to the hot-air balloon. Generally speaking, thinking about *anything* other than the negative or the problem is an improvement, but the most effective method of thought control is to strategically shift problem and negative thinking to "what can be done to improve" or any other solution-focused type of thinking.

The Scheeler family could have easily fallen into depression and crumbled after losing Mary. Instead, they reminded themselves often of the fact, "There is *always* a solution. *Always.*" And reminding themselves of this allowed them not to get stuck in thinking that there was nothing else to do but surrender to the grief. Later, we will cover the specifics of *how* to replace PCT with RSF, but for now, let's stay focused on *why* it is so important to do so.

CORTISOL OR SEROTONIN?
YOU CHOOSE

This is probably a good time to explain what happens biologically when you choose to focus on problems. Like it or not, anytime you allow your thoughts to zero in on problems or the negative aspects of life, your brain releases into your bloodstream the neurotransmitter known as cortisol. In small doses cortisol can be helpful; however, it becomes bad very quickly when increased amounts are released. Unfortunately, it takes only a small amount of PCT to overload the system with cortisol. And when I say this is bad, I mean this is really bad. Cortisol is the root of all negative emotion. Human beings do not possess the ability to experience negative emotions such as fear, anger, and stress without the release of cortisol into the bloodstream.

In addition to feeling bad, an overload of cortisol decreases all cognitive functioning. Translation: when you think about problems, you feel emotionally horrible, you become measurably more ignorant, and your likelihood of making bad decisions increases significantly. Think about the impact cortisol can have on a person over extended periods of time. We have an entire society of people walking around with elevated levels of cortisol, feeling totally stressed out and unaware of how to correct the issue.

Herein lies the true explanation for the current state of the human race. You need not be a genius to see that more and more people are cracking under the pressures of life. Road rage, school shootings, suicide, and other unthinkable acts have become part of the fabric of our society, and it can all be traced to cortisol breaking down the human spirit. Everyone has problems. Unfortunately, we are not taught how to deal with those problems effectively, so they grow into bigger and bigger problems.

In some cases, people are so unable to deal with those problems that they snap.

I realize this is some pretty heavy information; however, there is good news. There is something we can do about it, and that something is to commit to developing the RSF mindset. Doing so can and will change the world. The second a person stops thinking about problems and begins focusing on solutions, the brain stops releasing cortisol and begins releasing a whole new set of neurotransmitters: dopamine, serotonin, and norepinephrine. These neurotransmitters biologically cause us to feel happy and motivated. Immediately upon release of these neurotransmitters, we start feeling better, and we experience significant and measurable increases in intelligence, creativity, and energy.

Learning to focus on solutions through RSF helps us avoid feelings of negativity, hopelessness, and despair. Instead of becoming overwhelmed and creating negative cycles of existence, a person creates the conditions for hope and progress. Imagine for a moment a society of people filled with hope and ability, rather than individuals feeling overwhelmed, defeated, and hopeless.

The thoughts we choose to have dictate how we feel and behave. The RSF mindset is all about learning to choose thoughts that produce an increase in positive emotions and behaviors. Choosing the "correct" thoughts is essentially what mental toughness is all about. *Anything* solution-focused counts and promotes marked improvements in your quality of life. It is imperative that we take responsibility to commit to learning a better way to live.

The thoughts we choose to have dictate how we feel and behave.

HOW RSF WORKS

Let me offer a simple example of how different life can be when a person chooses the RSF mindset. I will use an area I am quite familiar with—Major League Baseball.

It's quite common to think about one problem, only to get sucked into the PCT tornado, eventually convincing yourself that you have nothing positive in your life at all. And yes, this absolutely happens, even with professional athletes.

First, let's consider a player who has not been trained in RSF. This player comes up to bat in the bottom of the seventh inning. The bases are loaded with two outs, and his team is down by one run. He eyes down the pitcher, gets his pitch, and . . . strikes out. As he walks back to the dugout to get his glove, he starts thinking to himself, "This is not good. This is the second time in two weeks I've struck out with the bases loaded. I just bought a second home that I'm not sure we can afford if I don't get a better Major League contract. If I keep playing like this, I'm not sure that I'll get a new contract at all. How in the heck am I going to explain this to my wife? What am I going to tell my kids? I'm a complete loser."

Here's the problem. When things aren't going your way, life won't let you call time-out so you can feel sorry for yourself. In fact, life has a nasty way of coming at you even harder in situations like this.

Now, this player is standing in the outfield, and he's thinking about that strikeout and how he's such a loser. Before he knows it, a player from the other team hits a long fly ball in his direction. He's not totally focused because he has all this negative stuff going on in his head. He doesn't get a good read on the ball, and he doesn't get a good jump. Keep in mind, this guy has all the heart in the world, so he takes off with 100 percent effort, sprinting to the corner, and he even lays out trying to make the catch . . . the ball bounces off his glove and rolls into the corner of the outfield. Now there's a man standing on second base, and his team is still losing by a run.

He goes back to his spot in the outfield, and the negative thoughts start taking over again. He starts telling himself, "Oh man, this really isn't good. I just struck out with the bases loaded, and on film it's probably going to look like I should've made that catch. I just bought a second home, and it's a contract year. I just really don't think I have put enough money away, and the way I am playing, I may not get that contract at all. How am I going to explain this to my wife? What am I going to tell my kids? I am a complete loser."

Then another fly ball comes his way, but PCT has distracted him again. Once he zeroes in, he takes off with 100 percent effort. He chases the ball into the corner, but once again he is unable to get to it in time. Now his team is down by two runs, and there is a new man standing on second base. *That which you focus on expands.*

Having worked with a number of MLB ballplayers, I can tell you that this situation is absolutely the reality, and while you might not be into baseball, surely you've had a situation similar to what this ballplayer was experiencing. Every person can relate to this scenario at some level. You strike out at one thing, and your mind starts focusing on that strikeout. Then the PCT tornado starts to swirl, and it sucks you in. The next thing you know, you have convinced yourself that you're a complete loser.

Let's compare this player to one who has gone through RSF training and invests time daily into training his brain to search for solutions. Same situation as the previous player, he comes up to bat in the bottom of the seventh inning with the bases loaded, two outs, and his team is losing by a run. He gets into the box, eyes down the pitcher, gets his pitch, and . . . strikes out. Keep in mind, RSF is not going to keep you from having problems. Having problems is a guaranteed part of our human experience. RSF teaches you how to more effectively deal with the problems that you are *guaranteed* to have.

After the strikeout, the player goes back to the dugout to get his glove and starts thinking, "This is not good. Second time in two weeks I've struck out with the bases loaded. I've got a contract year. . . ." (This is where the RSF shift begins. Instead of allowing himself to focus on the strikeout, he forces his thoughts to solutions.) The first step toward RSF is the player *recognizing* the beginning of PCT, and saying to himself, "I'm not going to go there." Then he works on *replacing* the PCT with RSF by asking himself one simple question: "What is one thing I can do right now that could make this better?" He looks down and sees that he's got a glove on his hand, and he says to himself, "Well, I guess I could focus on playing some defense!"

Now he's standing in the outfield, and he knows the only way not to think about the strikeout is to focus instead on a solution. He does not let his mind think about the strikeout, no matter how badly he wants to. He *forces* his mind to focus on the task at hand—playing solid defense. For him, his solution is to continually tell himself, "Track the ball, quick feet, follow through." He's standing in the outfield, and he *wants* to focus on that strikeout, but he won't allow it. In his head, he is forcing his mind to focus on tracking the ball. The pitcher is now standing on the mound with the ball in his hand and glove. The outfielder is tracking that ball as it leaves the pitcher's hand and is headed for the hitter. The outfielder is still tracking that ball. The ball makes contact with the hitter's bat, and he's in the outfield forcing his mind to continue to "track the ball." He gets a good read. Now it's time for "quick feet," and he gets a great jump. He chases the ball into the corner, with 100 percent effort he lays out, and this time . . . he makes a great catch.

Next, he goes back to his spot in the outfield, and guess where his mind wants to go? Remember, you will do 99 things right on any given day and one thing less than perfectly, and where does your mind go? This player is built just like you and me, and his mind naturally wants to go back to thinking about that strikeout.

PCT ensures that our minds find their way back to the negative, even in the face of a success. "Oh man, that was a great catch. If only I would have put the bat on the ball in the last inning, I'd probably have made ESPN. That's the second time I've struck out in the last two weeks with the bases loaded. I'm in a contract year. . . ." Again, the player *recognizes* he's falling back to PCT and he makes his mental shift, *"What is one thing I can do right now that could make this better?"*

Instead, he replaces the negative focus with the task at hand. "Track the ball, quick feet, follow through." Now here comes another long fly ball. He's tracking the ball, he gets another great jump, chases it into the corner, lays out, and . . . makes another great catch. Maybe he will even end up on *ESPN's Top 10*.

Like it or not, that is real life. That happens to every one of us. We may not be in the outfield of a Major League game anytime soon, but every day you are sitting in meetings, spending time with your kids, working on your fitness, hanging with your spouse, or anything else that our lives entail, that is the equivalent of you taking your at-bats, standing in the outfield, and making catches. The thing to remember is we choose whether or not we allow ourselves to focus on our problems or the solutions. We either win or lose each day; this is our choice, and it all begins with the thoughts in our heads.

We either win or lose each day; this is our choice, and it all begins with the thoughts in our heads.

CONTROL YOUR THOUGHTS; CONTROL YOUR BEHAVIORS

Many people allow themselves to believe that we don't have control over our behaviors. Like it or not, you have 100 percent control over whether you have that second piece of cake, whether you close those social media apps so you can finish preparing your presentation, or whether you wake up with the alarm to get your morning workout done. Some things are easier to control than others, for sure, but the first step to controlling those behaviors, even the most difficult ones, is accepting that they are your choice. The thoughts you choose will ultimately control your behaviors. I know some people reading this won't want to believe it, and some of you may have even been taught that what I am saying is incorrect. The "disease model" would suggest that there are certain behaviors that are fully dictated by something outside of your control. The disease model is accurate in approximately 10 percent of the population. Unfortunately, there are many who have profited by misdiagnosing people who biologically may have *difficulty* controlling behavior, but have been told they have *no* ability whatsoever to control those behaviors.

Think about this for a moment, how would you feel if a supposed "expert" in the field diagnosed you or your child with an inability for behavior control? It would be very easy to believe the diagnosis, and unfortunately, believing the diagnosis actually causes the diagnosis to become even more real. There are many medical professionals who should be ashamed of how loosely they throw certain diagnoses around. Not having to take responsibility for one's behaviors is far easier than being accountable, and in the end it is far more costly.

Controlling behaviors always begins with controlling thoughts. While there is no magic formula to prevent all negative thoughts from entering your mind, an extremely important element of behavior control has much to do with how long you allow the negative thoughts to swirl in your mind before shifting them to a solution. This is a good time to review the definition of RSF: within 60 seconds, replace all negative thinking with solution-focused thought. The sooner you can replace problem-focused thoughts with solution-focused thinking the better.

THE MOST IMPORTANT
60 SECONDS OF YOUR DAY

The magic number with RSF is 60. Sixty seconds. The faster you replace negative or problem-focused thinking with RSF, the less of a negative impact the cortisol has on your ability to make good decisions. Replacing problem-centric thoughts with solution-focused thinking within 60 seconds is critical to being able to make better decisions about what behaviors you should choose. Remember, increased levels of cortisol negatively impacts all cognitive functioning, and shifting away from PCT within 60 seconds helps keep the cortisol release under control. Allowing the problem focus for longer than 60 seconds is where many people lose the battle for good decision making and improved behavior control.

The 60-second marker was something I determined after years of study and work with clients and is a critical aspect of the execution of RSF. It is the meter for assessing whether we are breaking free from PCT effectively or not. Giving yourself a maximum of 60 seconds ensures that you have enough time to recognize that the negative thought cycle has begun, but not enough time for it to swirl out of control. The speed at which this switch to solution-focused thinking occurs is the key to escaping PCT before the negative neurotransmitters release into the bloodstream. It is important to understand that the longer you allow yourself to focus on problems, the harder it becomes to take control of your thoughts and move them to the solution zone.

I'd be willing to bet that you've already had someone say to you at one time or another, "Don't be negative," or, "Just be positive!" If it were this easy, everyone would be mentally tough, and RSF would be the norm. Truth be told, not very many people even believe that they *can* be mentally tougher. Remember the "I'm just not a morning person" excuse in Chapter 1? Some people may resist at first or think that there is no hope for their personal situation; however, you will find that whatever you work on, you will improve—and that includes mental toughness. If you want to get better at controlling your thoughts and behaviors, all you need to do is put some effort into working toward it.

Science confirms that you have it in you to learn to become more mentally tough. Neuroplasticity refers to our brain's ability to be molded and changed throughout our lifetime. Every human brain has plasticity—the ability to change. Through neuroplasticity, we can, in fact, retrain our brains so that RSF becomes more normal for us than PCT.

> **Neuroplasticity:** our brain's ability to be molded and changed throughout our lifetime

RECOGNIZE WHEN YOU NEED RSF— YOUR CRITICAL ALARM SYSTEM

These first three chapters have been designed to help you recognize when PCT is happening to you, which enables you to do something about it. Determining when you are actually allowing your brain to focus on problems is more difficult than you might expect—unless you know what to look for.

Unfortunately, most people have never been taught how to recognize the alarm that tells us that PCT is taking over. You see, our society has become so afraid of negative emotion that we will do anything to get rid of it as quickly as possible. We make excuses so we don't have to feel guilty. We take medicine so we don't have to feel anxiety. We blame others so we don't have to take accountability. We detach from the people who are important to us so we don't have to feel the pain they may cause us.

Remember, when PCT is happening, your brain releases neurotransmitters that make you feel like garbage. Negative emotion was not given to us as a curse—it was given to us as a gift. The only good thing about feeling like garbage is that it serves as your critical PCT alarm system. Anytime you feel negative emotion (stress, anxiety, fear, anger, depression, guilt—otherwise known as "the nasty six"), it is because your problem-focused thoughts have triggered the negative neurotransmitter release. Humans literally cannot experience those negative emotions unless PCT is happening. Anytime you experience a negative emotion, we want you to quickly recognize that you must be engaging in PCT. This alarm system is 100 percent effective at alerting you to your need for RSF.

Negative emotion is the "gift of recognition" that lets us become aware that our thoughts are problem focused and that to improve our quality of life, we need to get to work on solutions. It tells us that something is broken, and we need to fix it. It isn't possible to change the way you think unless you first can *recognize* when a change in thinking is necessary. From now on, anytime you feel negative emotion, this is your cue that you must replace your focus.

---

*Negative emotion is the "gift of recognition"
that lets us become aware that our thoughts are
problem focused and that to improve our quality
of life, we need to get to work on solutions.*

 THINGS TO *KNOW*

1. You must remember, "There is *always* a solution. *Always.*"
2. Thinking about problems causes a biological release of cortisol. Cortisol is responsible for all negative emotion (stress, anxiety, fear, anger, depression, or guilt). Anytime you experience any of these "nasty six" emotions, that is the 100 percent effective alarm that your focus is on a problem.
3. Relentless Solution Focus (RSF): Within 60 seconds, replace all problem-focused thinking with solution-focused thought.

THING TO *DO*

Take a moment now to assess where you are currently with RSF, without having completed any training. Give yourself a score on a scale of 1 to 10. If you are able to move from problem-thinking to a potential solution within 60 seconds 20 percent of the time throughout the day, your score would be a 2. If you are able to move to solution-thinking within 60 seconds 40 percent of the time, you would be a 4. Most people without any prior RSF training are typically about a 4. The purpose of this is not to beat yourself up for how poor you are at RSF—remember, it is typical to be bad at this. The purpose is to self-assess where your baseline is so that you can have a starting point for improvement.

PART II

REPLACE

If It's Broken, Fix It

4

The Mental Chalkboard

Solving the "Real" Problem

Kye Hawkins had a textbook pregnancy and a picture-perfect delivery with her son Max. She describes her biggest concerns during her pregnancy as choosing the perfect gender-neutral paint color for the nursery and making sure she had a onesie in every hue. But when Max was born, something wasn't right, and suddenly the paint color couldn't have mattered less. Upon his birth, Max was blue and appeared to be full of fluid, and he couldn't seem to take in a big breath or let out a big cry. After hours that felt like days waiting for answers, Max's family finally got the news that he had been born with posterior urethral valves (PUV), a rare blockage of the urethra in utero, which resulted in his kidneys and bladder essentially being poisoned to the point that they were rendered useless. He spent 69 agonizing days in the neonatal intensive care unit (NICU). The neonatal nephrology team in charge of Max stated that he was the most serious and complex case they had ever seen.

Max's parents spent those 69 days doing everything they possibly could to prepare for their new full-time jobs of caring for their child's needs. The next year included round-the-clock dialysis treatments and catheterizations to relieve Max's bladder, seven daily medications and injections, physical therapy, occupational therapy, and countless doctors' appointments. They knew that dialysis brings a kidney to only about 60 percent functionality and was not sustainable for the long term. Just as pressing were the developmental delays Max was experiencing as a result of not having a functioning kidney. Max would need a new kidney, but he would not even be able to get on the transplant list until he reached the height and weight requirements.

At 16 months old, he met the requirements for a transplant, and testing finally began to find a match for a new kidney. Kye had three cousins and a sister who were all matches and willing to give Max their kidney. At two-and-a-half years old, Max finally got his "shiny new kidney" from Kye's cousin, Kassidy, who was the perfect match. Kye told Ellen, "How glad I was to see that dialysis machine get packed up and leave our house. But also kind of sad, which sounds odd, but it did keep our son alive for over two years." Max is thriving and loving being a big brother to Kye and her husband's second son, Kip. Kye says,

> After spending his early years surrounded by and communicating directly with doctors, surgeons, and nurses, Max is at ease with adults and in adult conversations. It is really sort of a miracle for a kid who didn't really talk at all until he was three years old. He also loves to impersonate adults in their occupations: UPS delivery men and women, grocery clerks, teachers, doctors, veterinarians, landscapers. If he sees someone working, five minutes later, he is in full costume and impersonating him or her. We feel like children's theater is calling his name.

Of course, the story doesn't end there, as Max needs continuous care and eventually needs another kidney transplant later in his life. You get the idea—Max and his family experience struggle unlike most will ever experience.

The problem for Max and his family was obvious: he needed a new kidney. However, what they know that others don't is that the real problem isn't the problem itself, but rather how people deal with the problem. The real problem is that we have the biologically ingrained tendency to make our problems worse by focusing on them. Of course it's a problem to need a new kidney, just like it is to lose your job or go through a divorce or any other of life's challenges; however, what most people often forget is that problems are common. We all have them. The key to successfully navigating life is to realize that thinking about or focusing on our problems does nothing to solve them, but rather makes things worse. Much worse.

The real problem is that we have the biologically ingrained tendency to make our problems worse by focusing on them.

People who learned "Mighty Max's" story felt like they knew Max and his parents because Kye beautifully documented their journey online for any followers who might be interested, and Ellen followed their story. You might be thinking that this would be a sad story to follow, but it was quite the opposite. Yes, much of Max's life has consisted of surgeries, blood draws, and hospital stays; and there was setback after setback on Max's road to his shiny new kidney, but Kye managed to present their story as one of hope, joy, love, and celebration. Kye is not naive. She is not delusional to her reality. She is not in denial. She is optimistic—and I mean *relentlessly* optimistic. Kye told Ellen, "I've gotten some version of an 'optimism award' four or five times in my life—from the 'Glass Half Full!' paper plate at summer camp to the more meaningful Optimism Award from Education Pioneers, a fellowship I participated in during graduate school. It's within me, and it seems it always has been." Kye refuses to allow her problems to monopolize her thoughts or her life. Every time she catches herself going down the "poor me" road, she quickly changes her reality by turning her thoughts from the negative to either focusing on all the good things she has or solving whatever problem has presented itself. Kye is one of the most mentally tough people Ellen and I have come across.

I take no credit for Kye's mental toughness, but she is one of those people whom I appreciate so much because she teaches us how to be better. She is not running a multimillion-dollar corporation. She is not leading her team to the World Series. She's not climbing Mount Everest. What she is doing is so much bigger than those things. She's winning at life—plain ol' everyday life, in a big way. I don't mean in the "Wow, she's really made the best of her crappy situation" way. I mean *really* winning at life. Her family experiences love, joy, and happiness—so much so that many others cannot even begin to understand how that could be.

We share Kye and Max's story with you because it demonstrates the difference between how typical people view a situation versus how mentally tough people view a situation. Kye points out that one of the frustrating things that well-meaning people often say to her is: "I don't know how you do it!"

This might even be a phrase that you've uttered to someone else going through one of life's challenges. On the surface, it seems supportive, but when you really break this down, what people are actually saying is "Man, it would suck to be in your situation," and "I can't imagine being functional in a life so terrible." "I don't know how you do it" is an invitation to begin thinking and talking about problems. Of course, no one is consciously saying that to Kye, but that is essentially what that comment means. Kye says that is one of the only things that people say to her that really "stings." It's already hard enough to avoid PCT, we certainly don't need others trying to drag us back into it.

Unfortunately, she probably hears that phrase a lot. The reason for that is PCT. People are great at focusing on problems, and because of that, they expect others to be the same way. They may not understand how Kye and her family are able to handle—and even thrive with—the cards they've been dealt because most give in so easily to PCT.

THE REAL PROBLEM

Remember, the real problem isn't the actual problem. The real problem is that people don't recognize that the typical way of dealing with problems actually makes problems worse. *Don't be typical.* Your goal is to be better than typical, and you do that through Relentless Solution Focus (RSF).

What most people don't understand is that we actually get to choose our lot in life. We *can* choose our thoughts, which *cause* our emotions and behaviors. With training, our thoughts become our choice. Nothing and no one can choose for you. Only you are responsible for choosing for yourself. No matter how good or bad you have it, your thoughts are *always* your choice.

No matter how good or bad you have it,
your thoughts are always your choice.

We can choose to be stressed out, anxious, and angry, or we can choose to feel happy, in control, and energized. The human brain can fully focus only on one thing at a time. If we learn to focus on the positive or the potential solutions to our problems, this guarantees we will spend significantly less time focused on problems or negativity.

THE MENTAL CHALKBOARD

Imagine that our brains have a mental chalkboard with a line down the center dividing a problem side and a solution side. PCT ensures that we are experts at the problem side of the board. Not only do most people spend a large amount of time on this side of the mental chalkboard, they get sucked deeper and deeper into it because of expectancy theory. When we are on the problem side of the board, we actually *create* more and larger problems because *that which you focus on expands.*

PROBLEM	SOLUTION

It is common for Kye to hear some version of "I don't know how you do it," because most people live on the problem side of the mental chalkboard and have a hard time understanding how Kye doesn't. Whether this comes naturally to Kye or she's had to work at it, she is a wonderful example of the power of RSF.

"The Great Myth" and the Mental Chalkboard

Remember the *Great Myth* from Chapter 2? The great myth is the idea that talking about or thinking about your problems will lead you to a solution. This is why many people get stuck on the problem side of the mental chalkboard. Ellen had a client who came to her with the goal of becoming a partner in his advertising firm. He had been with the firm for more than 10 years, and he was already a couple of years behind where he wanted to be at this point in his life. He was frustrated that he had not become a partner within the past two years, and he found himself starting to flounder. During their first meeting, he presented his current situation to Ellen, and he spent some time describing how the leaders of the firm did not seem to have good ideas about where the firm should be going, and how they were not keeping up with the current technologies and cultural shifts. It quickly became clear to Ellen that he was an expert on the company's problems, and he was frustrated that the firm's leaders did not recognize that he could help fix them. He said, "A few colleagues that I really respect all agree that the current leadership has serious blind spots." Ellen recognized that this was code for, "We spend a lot of time talking about our problems."

Here is the thing about problems—they are really good at disguising themselves as important. People love to talk and vent about problems because it makes them feel like they understand something at a very deep level. It makes them feel smart without really having to take any accountability for them. That may sound harsh, but let me emphasize that the most successful and happiest people who sit in Ellen's or my office rarely sit there venting or complaining. They have learned that doing so is a complete waste of time. Oftentimes the most difficult part of the growth process is getting people to understand and admit to themselves how much time and energy they actually put into focusing on problems.

Ellen's client was smart, ambitious, and normal in terms of how he dealt with problems, but he had to go to work on the "normal" part to get past his current plateau. He actually considered firing Ellen a number of times, and he admitted to thinking that "She obviously doesn't understand what it takes to succeed at this level." Fortunately, Ellen's reputation of high-level success in the professional sports world and corporate America gave this client enough confidence to continue taking this new way of thinking on a "test-drive."

Ellen pushed him to keep a drawing of the mental chalkboard on his desk. Anytime he would catch himself feeling frustrated with leadership or undervalued, he would write the issue down on the "problem" side of the chalkboard. But he wasn't allowed to stop there. Anytime something went up on the problem side, he knew he had to come up with something he could do in that moment to make it better. Sometimes that meant refocusing his attention on his most important tasks, sometimes that meant jotting down three things that he had done well that day, and sometimes that meant volunteering to take on a task that would help move a project forward.

The rule was, "last thought positive." No matter what, if he identified a problem or something he didn't like, he had to put a potential solution up on that mental chalkboard. There would be no excuse accepted for not doing so. The client later admitted that Ellen's intolerance for excuses increased his confidence in her and was a big part of his decision to keep her as a coach.

Here's the important thing to remember: Ellen's client's biggest problem wasn't that his leadership wasn't running the company correctly. His biggest problem was that he was living on the problem side of the mental chalkboard, and it was consuming his energy, productivity, and creativity—it was sucking the joy out of his job. What he hadn't realized was that *he* was the one taking himself farther and farther from his goal by living on the problem side. PCT is sneaky like that.

He came into Ellen's office thinking he was going to leave with a 12-step plan for getting ahead at his firm, but what he left with was a simple drawing of the mental chalkboard. He also gave himself the rule that he wasn't allowed to discuss frustrations with others. We like to discuss frustrations and vent to others because we know they will join us on the problem side and keep us company—we are good at helping each other become better at being worse. When he wasn't allowed to discuss his frustrations, one of two things happened: (1) his frustration or problem dissipated quickly when he avoided adding fuel to his PCT fire, or (2) he was forced to come up with solutions to those problems that didn't just go away on their own.

By keeping the mental chalkboard at the forefront of his mind, he started to show up at work every day with more energy, he was more productive, and he was doing things that were actually getting noticed by his leadership—so much so that he is now in conversations about a partnership at his firm.

Cross the Line and Stop Drinking the Poison

To have an RSF mindset means you consistently get to the solution side of the mental chalkboard within 60 seconds, and you are relentless about staying there. The key is to cross the line. Always finish on the solution side. Remember, when a person is on the problem side of the mental chalkboard, the brain is releasing cortisol into the bloodstream. You already know that cortisol causes you to feel like garbage (stress, anxiety, anger, fear, depression, and guilt), and it limits creativity, intelligence, and happiness. This is a biological process, and you can't stop it from happening. This is literally like drinking poison, and many of us do this on a consistent basis.

To have an RSF mindset means you consistently get to the solution side of the mental chalkboard within 60 seconds, and you are relentless about staying there.

The good news—the poison is not very strong. The bad news—even though it is a low-dose poison, it still adds up. This is exactly why people who don't work on RSF are significantly more likely to experience poor health and on average die 14 years sooner. Yes, you just read the last sentence correctly. People with RSF live up to 14 years longer than typical people. Not only do they live longer, they are significantly happier, healthier, and more successful.

The second you cross the center line of that mental chalkboard, your brain begins releasing a whole new set of neurotransmitters—dopamine, serotonin, and norepinephrine. These biologically cause us to feel happy and motivated. Immediately upon crossing the line from the problem side to the solution side of the board, we start feeling better and experience a significant and measurable increase in intelligence, creativity, and energy.

People with RSF live up to 14 years longer than typical people. Not only do they live longer, they are significantly happier, healthier, and more successful.

Remember, to cross the line from problem to solution, we must first be able to *recognize* when we are on the problem side to begin with. What I have found is that we are fairly good at recognizing when *other* people are on the problem side of the board, but when it comes to ourselves, it is a whole lot more difficult for us to self-assess. In fact, right now you may be thinking how you wish some people you know were reading this book because they are always on the problem side of the board. Don't take this the wrong way, but they may be thinking the same thing about you. Let me say it again, it's actually quite easy to recognize when someone else is on the wrong side of the mental chalkboard, but being problem-focused is so typical for us that we often overlook it when we ourselves are there.

Remember, when you feel any negative emotion, that is your cue that you are in fact on the PCT side of your mental chalkboard. You cannot experience stress, anxiety, fear, anger, depression, or guilt (the nasty six) without the PCT trigger.

Dan is a financial advisor who came to Ellen a few years ago to help him get to the next level of production. He was already bringing in close to $750,000 in revenue each year, but he had his sights set on becoming a million-dollar producer. He was obviously already doing a lot of things well, but they focused on small ways he could become more efficient and productive. They'd been working together for several months, and he was experiencing good results, but lately his results had stalled a bit. He knew he needed to get in more daily client phone calls, but he didn't know how to find the time in his schedule. Ellen asked him to walk her through his morning routine, knowing that many people waste a lot of time "settling in" when first arriving at work. Dan began, "Well, first, I take two Xanax to help get me ready to make my phone calls, then I like to wait about 20 minutes or so for it to kick in, so then I check some emails and browse through the paper before I start on the phone."

This was the first time he had mentioned the need for anti-anxiety medication to her, and he said it so casually that it was almost like he was talking about brushing his teeth. She asked him to tell her more about the need for Xanax. He said, "I have anxiety in the mornings before I start my day, and the Xanax helps me feel ready to make my phone calls."

Ellen asked Dan to dig into this a bit more, to think about what provokes anxiety in him in the mornings. You see, Dan was so quick to try to get rid of his anxiety that he hadn't stopped to think about what the anxiety was really telling him. He went on to say, "Well, I guess it's the feeling that I don't really know what's going to happen when I start talking to people. I can't control what they are going to say, or whether the calls are going to go the way I want." Dan's anxiety was an alarm that was alerting him to the fact that on some level his mind didn't feel prepared for his morning. The feeling of lack of control manifested as anxiety. He was putting a Band-Aid on a bullet hole. Yes, he was somewhat effectively controlling the symptoms, but in doing so, he was keeping himself from addressing the cause.

Your body doesn't feel *anything* unless your mind tells it to. Nothing happens without our brains first directing it. Dan's anxiety was a clue that he was focused on a problem—he didn't feel prepared for what his day would bring. Instead of coming up with a solution to the real problem, he was silencing the alarm with Xanax.

Your body doesn't feel anything
unless your mind tells it to.

Now, I am not discounting the benefit of medication for some cases, but I can't tell you the number of frustrated people who have come into our office after seeing therapist after therapist only to find the answer to their anxiety or depression in RSF. Biological depression occurs in roughly 10 percent of the population, yet a 2016 NBC news report showed that roughly one in six Americans was taking antidepressants and that each year those numbers were increasing. That means more than 40 million people are taking medication unnecessarily. Let me explain how this happens. If you go into a psychiatrist's office and complain of stress or anxiety, what do you think the chances of being prescribed meds are? Close to 100 percent. Psychiatrists are trained in the medical model. This means their training has been solely focused on treating symptoms with medication, so of course that is the action they take. Just as if you come into Ellen's or my office, there is a 100 percent chance you will be given "talk therapy" as a course of action.

It is concerning to me that many people like Dan have been instructed by physicians to take antidepressants or anti-anxiety medication, just as they would take a couple of ibuprofen for a headache. I want to be crystal clear on my views of medication.

Of course, I know for some, it is the difference-maker and necessary. However, taking meds has become a pacifier for the mind for many. Taking medication may feel like a solution, but it does nothing to stop the problem from occurring day after day. Learning to develop the RSF mindset breaks this chain.

The truth is, most people have never been taught how to effectively reduce stress and anxiety without the use of medication. For 90 percent of the population, it really is as simple as learning to control your thoughts. For the other 10 percent, this is a tremendously helpful tool that works in cooperation with medication. Every person benefits from learning how to develop the RSF mindset.

I don't want you to view negative emotion as a bad thing or as something to avoid at all cost. Instead, learn to see it for what it is. It's the message your body is sending back to your brain that it's time for a change. Instead of living on the problem side of the mental chalkboard, it is time to move over to the solution side. Negative emotion is definitely uncomfortable, so use it as motivation to begin replacing negative thoughts with solution-focused thinking. Changing thoughts changes behaviors; changing behaviors changes results.

Changing thoughts changes behaviors; changing behaviors changes results.

Being aware of the mental chalkboard better positions a person to replace those negative thoughts with much more positive and helpful thinking. The next chapter will begin to outline *how* to replace those nasty problem-centric thoughts with the type of thinking that will change your life for the better, using the RSF tool. The RSF tool has been proven to effectively help move a person from the problem side of the mental chalkboard to the solution side, and to do so within 60 seconds or less.

③ THINGS TO *KNOW*

1. The "real" problem isn't the actual problem itself. The real problem is that the typical way of dealing with problems actually makes problems worse. The longer we spend on the problem side of the mental chalkboard, the worse our problems become.
2. *Crossing the line* from the problem side to the solution side of the mental chalkboard is the key. We stop poisoning our bodies and minds with harmful neurotransmitters and start releasing ones that promote health, happiness, and success as soon as we cross the line.
3. It's common to think that you do not spend as much time on the problem side of the mental chalkboard as others do. No matter how often you are actually allowing yourself to be on the problem side of things, you always have an obligation to get yourself to the solution side within 60 seconds.

① THING TO *DO*

Create your own drawing of the mental chalkboard. On a piece of paper, draw a line vertically down the middle, and write "Problem" on the left and "Solution" on the right.

PROBLEM	SOLUTION

For the next 24 hours, keep this piece of paper on your desk, your kitchen table, your nightstand, or wherever you will see it frequently. Anytime you catch yourself feeling stressed, anxious, annoyed, or any other negative emotion, take a few seconds (but no more than 60) and recognize on the left side what problem you are focused on that is causing that emotion. Then write down on the solution side one thing you could do to begin attacking the problem. Remember, it doesn't necessarily need to solve your problem, but rather just make the situation even slightly better. This isn't an exercise in solving your problems, but rather on *crossing the line*. You win in life anytime you cross the line by shifting your thoughts from problems to potential solutions.

At the end of the 24 hours, if you experienced zero negative emotions (unlikely), then you will have nothing written down on the problem side. The much more likely scenario, however, is that you will have at least a few things written down. You may even have written down the same problem multiple times if you found your mind going back to it time and time again. It is very easy to get caught up ruminating on what has got you down. Don't allow yourself more than 60 seconds on the problem side before crossing the line and quickly jotting down some sort of potential solution on the solution side. It does not need to be perfect.

This exercise enables you to better recognize where your thoughts are and that you *can* choose better thoughts.

5

The RSF Tool

Failure Fades When
Quitting Isn't an Option

Mark McLean did not have a typical childhood. He was born in 1974 in middle America. Both his parents were raging alcoholics. His mother used to lock herself in the house to avoid being disturbed so she could drink a gallon of whatever booze was on sale that day. Mark and his two brothers would come home from school, find the doors locked, and take that as their cue to drop their backpacks and head off to play until late in the evening. Mark's father had schizophrenia and was in and out of mental institutions all throughout Mark's childhood. His father was always unpredictable and usually severely violent. Mark used to pick fights with his father to keep his mother and brothers from taking the beatings. Mark did this because he knew he could handle it better than the others. Although the bruises and cuts hurt, he knew he would heal.

School did not come easily for Mark, and he certainly did not enjoy it. In fact, he went to great lengths to avoid it. Mark had severe dyslexia, which made reading and writing nearly impossible for him. This was back in the 1980s, before traditional schools were equipped to diagnose and manage dyslexia. Although Mark wanted to learn and tried to figure out how, he didn't fit in. After another year of missing more than 100 days of school, getting into several fights, and being classified as a lost cause, the high school's administration forced Mark to leave. Mark was deemed one of the top 25 most at-risk kids of his district, and he was forced to attend a new experimental school for troubled kids. At this point in Mark's life, drugs and alcohol had consumed most of his waking moments. It would be a complete understatement to say Mark was in a bad situation.

Around this time, Mark's mother was getting sober and had decided to divorce his father. She had only one rule—no drugs or alcohol allowed in the house. Mark made it one month before his mother threw him out of the house to live on his own.

While other kids his age were learning the fundamentals of trigonometry and the basics of writing an English paper, Mark was figuring out how to survive. He learned how to steal gas and to secure food and shelter. He set up camp in a wooded area behind his school, and when he wasn't able to sleep at a friend's house, he would hunker down under the stars. He watched the weather reports so he would know when it would be raining or too cold to sleep outside. He learned that Dunkin' Donuts threw out their old donuts at 11:45 p.m., and that if he met the worker at the back door, it would save him from diving in the dumpster.

Throughout the next year, Mark learned fast. He learned tenacity and to never give up. He learned to put one foot in front of the other and to hold his head up even on the tough days— especially on the tough days—and he learned he was a fighter. He learned that if he was going to make it, he was going to have to harden his mind. For Mark, this was when he started developing what he called his "bulletproof mentality."

Although Mark didn't spend much time thinking about where he ultimately wanted to end up in life, he did know that he wanted something better for himself. He looked forward to the day when he could feel stable and in control. He even wanted a family of his own someday. He wouldn't follow in his father's footsteps. Instead, he would be the kind of dad he yearned for—a loving and caring man who took care of his family.

Mark refused to let himself get too disappointed with what he didn't have; rather, he focused on getting through each day and finding ways to make his tomorrow a bit better. When faced with a problem, his mind would instinctively be reminded of what his grandfather had taught him: "The only person who can take you out of the fight is you. You're never out of the fight." In other words, you never fail as long as you keep fighting.

Mark wasn't looking for perfection, just improvement. He knew that if he could just make it through each day, survival became a bit more likely. Surviving was success.

At the age of 19, for the first time in his life, he sat down and created goals for where he wanted to be in 1 year, 5 years, and 10 years. Mark knew he wanted to be a veterinarian. He wanted his own apartment and a reliable car.

"The only person who can take you out of the fight is you. You're never out of the fight."

At 20 years old, he took a job at Washington University School of Medicine as a janitor cleaning up after lab animals. Well, he referred to himself as a "janitor" because it was a little more glamorous than his actual job title of husbandry assistant, which meant he was the assistant to the guy who cleaned up the animal feces. He hated the job. But every day for two years he showed up and never complained or made excuses. "I remember volunteering in the surgical lab the night of my twenty-first birthday, thinking about all my friends' twenty-first birthdays. Not sad, but fixed on my markers and knowing my pathway is always going to be harder than others', and it's nobody's fault. Just is what it is." It would be normal for Mark to focus on all the hits he had taken in life and be consumed with anger and resentment, but he wasn't. There were probably plenty of people to blame for his problems, but he didn't focus on them. No one would have been surprised if Mark had become just another person who made bad choices and didn't make it. Mark decided early on that wasn't going to happen to him.

He wanted more for himself, so after working all day as a husbandry assistant, he took it upon himself to show up in the lab and learn as much as he could about anesthesia and anatomy. He learned how to wash surgical dishes and how to put in and take out sutures.

With his newly acquired skills and tremendous work ethic, Mark found success in the lab. He was promoted to animal technician, and then promoted again to research technician, and again to senior research technician.

He would revisit his goals every year, scratch out ones he had achieved, change those he no longer wanted, and add new ones. He continuously reminded himself, "The only person who can take you out of the fight is you. You're never out of the fight."

By the time Mark left Washington University School of Medicine, he had achieved many of his goals while becoming quite skilled in the medical field. He was now able to assist with animal heart transplants, run a surgical lab, and complete data analysis on histology protocol for staining heart tissue. Mark's skills reached such heights that he was asked by colleagues to help write articles on medical findings. Mark coauthored eight articles that were published in highly respected medical journals, and he even presented his clinical findings at a medical conference in front of thousands. Keep in mind, this is someone who barely finished high school.

Mark eventually took a job in medical sales and immediately loved it. During this time, he started another set of goals—his personal goals. Mark realized he wanted to start a family. In 2000 he met his wife, Emily, and a year and a half later they were married. They eventually had two beautiful children, Gavin and Maisie.

Mark applied for a job at ResMed, the global giant of enhanced sleep products, where he had made enough connections to get an interview for a managerial sales position. If he were to get this job, his yearly income would be larger than he'd ever thought possible.

After 20 hours of interviews, Mark was asked to fly to San Diego to meet with the ResMed leadership team. If things went well, he knew he might actually have a chance to meet with the CEO of the company, Keith Serzen.

Unfortunately for Mark, things weren't looking good. He knew on paper he wouldn't match up to the other candidates, so he would need to find a way to stand out. He caught the last flight out of St. Louis and landed in San Diego sometime after 7:30 p.m. This gave him plenty of time to secure a place to stay and be ready for his interview the next morning at 9:00 a.m. The trip did not begin well. American Airlines lost his bags. He was wearing boots, old worn-out jeans, and a "somewhat" clean T-shirt. By the time Mark realized his bags were lost, every clothing store in San Diego was closed and wouldn't open in time for his interview. Showing up late to the interview or without a suit was not how he wanted to stand out.

Mark hunkered down for the evening and awoke early on a quest to somehow get a suit, tie, dress shirt, and shoes before the interview. He positioned himself in the parking lot outside Macy's department store and waited. He knew, with some luck, he might be able to convince someone to open early to make a big sale.

The Macy's store manager arrived early at 7:30 a.m., and Mark told him his story and pleaded with him until the man finally unlocked the doors, 90 minutes before the store officially opened. He bought the only suit he could afford and had the salesman safety-pin it, so it would almost look like it actually fit. He hoped the oversized suit wouldn't be too much of an obstacle.

Mark arrived early for his interview and patiently waited his turn. Once he was called into the meeting, he was as open and genuine as he could be. Executive after executive was shocked and impressed with Mark's story, and after seven hours of interviews, he found himself face to face with Keith Serzen, the CEO.

Keith took one look at Mark and then another at his résumé and simply asked, "How in the world did you end up in my office?" The CEO looked again at Mark and his résumé and said, "On paper you are not qualified for this job; however, the fact that you made it into my office tells me all I need to know about you. You're hired."

His first year on the job, Mark crushed his quota and was the runner-up to the "Rookie of the Year." In his years with ResMed, he made the President's Club (top 8 percent) three times and was named National Account Manager of the Year in 2010.

When I asked Mark to share a few things he had learned in corporate America, here's how he responded: "Always help others. You never know when you'll need their help. There is always more than one way to obtain your goals—even when it doesn't look like it. Present solutions, not problems." He then went on to share his favorite quote by Thomas Edison: "Our greatest weakness lies in giving up. The most certain way to succeed is always to try just one more time."

Mark had so many opportunities to live on the problem side of the mental chalkboard—set up camp, dig in, and never leave. He had every excuse to look at the hand he was dealt and say, "Success is just not in the cards for me." Trying "just one more time" as Edison said sounds easy, right? But how many people would try after taking blow after blow after blow? Not many. That is what makes Mark relentless.

In 2015, during Mark's upward climb with ResMed, there was another problem. In his position as manager of hospitals—North America, he was making more money than he ever thought possible, but he was traveling 20 days every month. Mark knew he wasn't living up to his responsibilities as a husband and father. He found himself making excuses at home more and more. He decided he had one shot at raising his kids, and he was going to step up no matter the cost.

Mark asked for and received a demotion. Now this is something you do not do in corporate America. This is what we call "career suicide." It turns out that it was not career suicide for Mark. It was just a demotion, and it was the right move for him and his family. Mark McLean has been relentless in his efforts to be a great husband and father. His favorite lesson to his children is "The only person who can take you out of the fight is you. You're never out of the fight."

I asked Mark where he learned to be relentless.

> I don't think there's one thing that I can point back to. There are many battles in life, and each battle requires me to "switch on." I believe this comes from taking my toughest life experiences and using them as evidence, fuel, and a compass to allow me to mentally "switch on." I then recall all the times that I had been in tough situations, only to come out on the other end—sometimes better, sometimes worse, but always more experienced. I will be fine, even if I fail. For me, laying out the entire pathway from beginning to end gives me tunnel vision. I found if I can focus on one marker or stepping-stone at a time, I don't get overwhelmed. This allows me to approach the next marker with fresher ideas gained from my previous marker, without pre-formed ideas of how stuff has to be done. I also use the successes of each marker as fuel to strengthen my will and "never give up" attitude. It's my "bulletproof mentality."

For years, I have been fascinated with what causes an individual like Mark McLean to succeed. Someone who, for all practical purposes, should have failed in life. He didn't have any training on how the brain works or in the Relentless Solution Focus (RSF) mindset. Frankly, he didn't need it. There was something inside of him, something he was born with, that instinctively drove him to be relentless. To *never* give up. I think most of us recognize that there is always someone out there who has it worse. We all have seen or heard about those inspirational people in the world who overcome all odds, push through adversity, and reach unimaginable heights. But what about us mere mortals—the ones who weren't born with supreme grit and a never-quit attitude tattooed into our DNA?

SOME ARE JUST BORN WITH IT— THE REST OF US MUST LEARN IT

The pattern I see with the most mentally tough individuals is they know full well problems will occur. Not to say they borrow trouble before adversity strikes, but they are not surprised when difficulty presents itself. They are prepared for the worst, but plan for the best. Those who are most successful designate a small amount of time to figure out what is the worst that can happen, and what will be done to succeed in that scenario. Then, for the most part, they keep their minds focused on how they want life to go and what is needed to make that happen. When you have a solution for the worst-case scenario, all other solutions become easier. When you are *relentless* about solutions, you literally become unstoppable. In essence, focusing on solutions is mental toughness, and being relentless about it is the master key to success.

If you are a pitcher and the bases are loaded, and the best hitter in baseball is standing in the batter's box, it's quite common to think about the players on base and the fact that this guy hit a home run last time up. Or if you have a big presentation at work, your laptop crashed, and you didn't sleep last night, it's quite common for you to focus on how anxious you are that you will blow your big opportunity. Remember, this is PCT trying to keep you swirling around the problem side of your mental chalkboard.

Adversity itself isn't controllable. What is *always* controllable is what you *do* about it. The mentally tough zero in on what can be done—the solution side of the mental chalkboard. Instead of letting the problem create a sense of helplessness, the mentally tough choose to be relentless and take control. Effectively replacing PCT with the RSF mindset requires that a person gain control of her situation by first and foremost getting control of what is going on between the ears. Allow yourself to realize, "Yes, things could go wrong, and if they do, this is what I will do about it." After that, keep your focus on how you want it to go, and what you will need to do to make that happen.

Problems don't always come in the form of movie-worthy adversity. My first experience with RSF happened 15 years ago. We had just moved into our new home, it was a hot summer day, and I was out mowing the lawn. As I pushed the mower back and forth, my mind began focusing on the small but numerous brown patches of grass in my yard. I don't think anyone would have looked at my yard and even noticed those brown spots, but to me they were everywhere. The more I looked for them, the more I saw. I then looked over at my neighbor's yard, and his grass looked lush and green. There were even diagonal mow marks that you might see at the ball park. This made my focus deepen on my brown grass. I began to think to myself, "Why isn't my yard as nice and green as my neighbor's?"

As I continued mowing, the negative thoughts amplified, "I put a significant amount of effort into having a nice yard, and this is the best I can do? What if this is how the rest of my life will go? Even with my best effort, am I going to come up short?" The more I mowed, the more frustrated and concerned I became. And the negative thoughts kept swirling, "What if this is how it goes with my private practice? Do I really have the ability to help people? Will my results be inconsistent and average at best?" A pit was forming in my stomach as my anxiety rose. At the pinnacle of my negative thinking, I had myself convinced I was going to be unsuccessful in my business, and my wife and children would know I was a failure. I literally had made myself sick.

Yes, I know it may seem silly to get so worked up over brown grass, but at this point, my problem had moved well beyond brown grass. PCT had blown it up into something that was barely recognizable from the original issue. I was deep into the problem side of my mental chalkboard without even realizing it.

Then as my mowing continued, something changed my life forever. One simple question appeared in my mind: "What is one thing I can do that could make this (brown grass) better?" My first response was: "I don't know." I knew from my counseling education that "I don't know" was the one response that was not allowed. Saying "I don't know" immediately stops all potential growth, and I knew from hours of working with clients that "I don't know" gets you absolutely nowhere in life. I had learned a technique called the "Can't Say I Don't Know" game that I had used successfully with clients over the years. When I asked a question to which a client responded "I don't know," I would say,

> Let's play a game. It's called "Can't Say I Don't Know." The rules are fairly simple: I will ask you a question and if you respond with "I don't know" or anything that approximates "I don't know," then I score a point. If you come up with any answer at all other than "I don't know," then you score a point. First one to score a point wins the game.

Typically, this is all it took to get a person to push past not answering my questions.

I returned to the question, refusing to say "I don't know" this time. My first potential solution came to mind. I could hire a lawn company. I quickly rejected that idea because I actually enjoyed mowing back then. I could be outside and get a break from the toddlers running rampant in the house, not to mention that I couldn't afford to pay someone else to do the work. I asked the question again, "What is one thing I can do that could make this (brown grass) better?" I hate to admit it, but this time my focus actually shifted to my neighbor's yard, and I flippantly considered sabotaging it. Maybe if his yard didn't look so nice, mine wouldn't look so bad? Thankfully, I quickly dismissed the idea of "gassing" my neighbor's yard, as I knew it was wrong, and it would surely make me feel worse.

Again I asked the question, "What is one thing I can do that could make this (brown grass) better?" After a couple solutions that failed to seem result-worthy, it became very tempting for me to say, "I don't know" again, or "This problem just doesn't have a solution." That is what most of us would easily default to at this point in dealing with a problem, but that is not relentlessness, and that is not mental toughness. Not allowing myself to say, "I don't know," this time I focused on self-education. I could get a book on lawn care, or even better, research on the internet for help. After considering this, I wasn't crazy about those ideas because they seemed inefficient and time-consuming. I would need to figure out exactly what grass I had and find the specifics for the St. Louis climate. Again, I asked the question, "What is one thing I can do that could make this (brown grass) better?"

What if I were to take a six-pack of beer to my neighbor and ask him for some advice on how he cares for his yard? This time my answer stuck.

I finished mowing, took a shower, went to the grocery store, and picked up a six-pack of Heineken (his favorite beer), and with a notepad in hand, knocked on his door. We sat for about 30 minutes, and he helped me identify the solution. If you are curious, my problem was that I was "bagging" my grass, and instead I needed to be "mulching" it. This one little change helped reduce the brown spots significantly. I never did get to a point where my yard was as nice as my neighbor Dan's; however, there were many times over the years, I would catch myself looking at the yard and smiling at just how good it did look.

Your problems don't need to be huge to have the power to destroy your happiness and success. Sometimes they are just as unimportant as brown grass. PCT can turn your brown grass into a much bigger problem unless you have a concrete tool to combat it. That question that I asked myself repeatedly when dealing with my brown grass became the most important I have ever asked myself, and it now serves countless others as the RSF tool.

BE RELENTLESS WITH THE RSF TOOL

To effectively replace PCT with solutions, you must become very familiar with the RSF tool. The RSF tool comes in the form of that simple and proven question, and if answered, it efficiently shifts one's focus from problems to solutions. *"What is one thing I can do that could make this better?"* And remember, "I don't know" is not an answer. Once you make asking the RSF tool question a habit, it enables you to gain control over your thoughts and effectively and relentlessly defeat PCT.

> **RSF tool:** *"What is one thing I can do that could make this better?"*

For the pitcher facing the best hitter in baseball, the answer to this question might be to keep his pitches "low and inside." For the businesswoman whose laptop crashed before her sales presentation, it is to "present the facts, and ask for the order." The critical point is that no matter what your problem is, large or small, work to become relentless at searching for and identifying solutions using the RSF tool. Doing so will undeniably make your life one of constant growth and fulfillment.

To understand how to apply the RSF tool to your own problems, let's go back to the mental chalkboard.

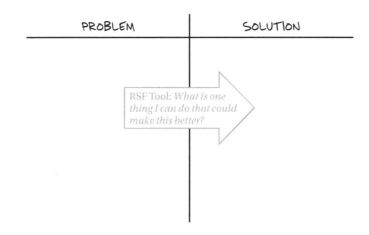

Anytime you find yourself on the problem side of the mental chalkboard, you can and should use the RSF tool to get yourself to the solution side within 60 seconds. Ask yourself that one simple question: *"What is one thing I can do that could make this better?"* Answering forces you to immediately cross over the line from the problem side of your board to the solution side. Quite simply, the RSF tool puts you back in control. It is a concrete method for shifting from PCT to RSF. Just as I did when I was dealing with my brown grass, often you need to use the RSF tool repeatedly until you get a solution that sticks (that is what it means to be relentless). Until that happens, you may bounce back and forth between the problem side and the solution side of the mental chalkboard. The key is to be relentless about not allowing yourself to *stay* on the problem side for more than 60 seconds. To get back to the solution side, you must use the RSF tool as many times as it takes: *"What is one thing I can do that could make this better?"*

Choosing the right thoughts by using the RSF tool keeps you in the fight. Anything less and the fight is over. This is precisely why *recognizing* PCT is paramount. Remember, when you catch yourself experiencing any negative emotion, that is your signal that you are on the problem side of your mental chalkboard. If you don't have the conscious awareness that you are focused on a problem and that doing so is really unproductive, there is no trigger or motive to replace the normal PCT current.

Here is a visual of my mental chalkboard when I was dealing with my brown grass. I bounced back and forth from the problem side to the solution side of my mental chalkboard several times before I ultimately found a solution that allowed me to stay on the solution side (take beer to my neighbor).

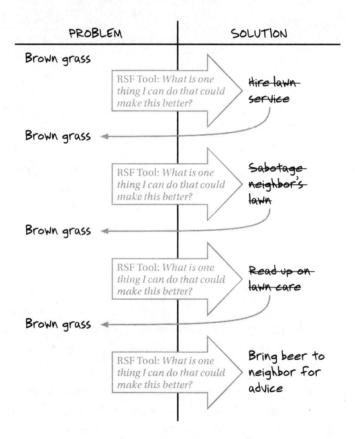

Every time I landed back on the problem side, I used the RSF tool to get me back over to the solution side. It doesn't matter how many times you bounce back to the problem side as long as you use the RSF tool to come up with a new solution each time. The key is to be relentless about getting back to the solution side as quickly as possible (ideally within 60 seconds). Keep your mental chalkboard in mind when working through your own problems using the RSF tool.

Be very clear on this point: the RSF tool doesn't have you asking yourself for five or three or even two things at a time to improve, but rather just *one* different action. And it doesn't ask you to identify the one *perfect* solution, but rather one potential *improvement*. When working through my brown grass problem, I came up with one solution at a time, and I didn't move on to coming up with a new solution until I had decided the previous solution would not help.

Think about Mark McLean. He did not allow himself to focus on the entirety of a bad situation. He knew doing so would only make things worse. Instead, he controlled adversity by getting his mind focused on what he could do to make things better— one problem at a time, and one solution at a time. He focused on the one thing daily that would keep him in the fight, and he was relentless about *always* having an answer to the RSF question.

GETTING ONE THAT STICKS

When we find ourselves on the problem side of the mental chalkboard, we must *force* ourselves to use the RSF tool and *continue* to come up potential solutions until one "sticks." Sometimes the first solution works. If so, great! If not, we have to go back to the drawing board (i.e., the mental chalkboard) one solution at a time, relentlessly, until either the situation is improved, or we have come up with a way to emotionally handle the situation differently.

This is where being relentless is critical. A typical person comes across a problem, tries a couple of different solutions, and gives up when solutions don't come easily or when complete resolution is not achieved. When most of us don't get immediate relief from our problems, we tell ourselves some version of, "Poor me. My problem is just too big. I give up." That is not relentlessness. You must continue the process until you have a solution on your mental chalkboard that you believe in. Without a solution, your mind has no way of staying in the RSF mindset and defaults back to PCT. Answering the RSF question is like dropping an anchor on the solution side. The potential solution keeps you on the healthy side of thinking. Remember, when your thoughts are focused on solutions, your brain isn't releasing those unhealthy neurotransmitters that wreak havoc on us mentally, physically, and emotionally.

Even if your problems aren't going away completely, there is a huge health benefit to merely looking through the solution-focused lens at life. Making small incremental improvements, even if it's only one inch at a time, keeps you living on the solution-focused side of the mental chalkboard. The goal is not necessarily to *solve* your problems, but rather to *improve* your situation and to *stay on the solution side* of the mental chalkboard.

There are problems in life that cannot be solved, but every situation can be improved. Improvements are solutions. Remember, there is always a solution. Always. The search should be for something—anything—that *improves* the situation, even if that means improving how you deal with the emotions the problem is causing. The solution does not have to be perfect. Just better.

The goal is not necessarily to solve *your problems, but rather to* improve *your situation and to* stay on the solution side *of the mental chalkboard.*

Solution: any improvement, even one inch, to the current situation

TWO TYPES OF SOLUTIONS

There are two types of solutions: solutions of action and solutions of inaction. Solutions of action are acceptable; solutions of inaction are not. Waiting for your problems to solve themselves is how most people deal with adversity. Some version of, "Sooner or later, this too shall pass" is a common mindset. As much as the old adage may be true, it is not the most effective way to thrive in life.

A pattern I have seen with highly successful people is what I refer to as the "attack mentality." Having an attack mentality means there is always one thing you are trying to improve. It's not trying to improve everything all the way all the time, but rather consistently working to have one thing you are trying to improve by just a little bit.

Those with the attack mentality don't wait for life to get better. They make life get better. This is the exact opposite of having a victim mentality. A person goes from having a victim mentality to an attack mentality by picking *one thing* to work on improving, and then getting all over that one thing. Even if the chosen action is a mistake or misdirection, inevitably improvements will come more quickly and frequently than waiting for things to improve on their own. Being relentless is all about taking action.

Let me illustrate this point with one of my favorite stories of relentlessness. At 8:00 a.m. on Friday, October 13, 1972, Nando Parrado and 44 of his rugby teammates left an Uruguayan Air Force base on a twin turboprop plane, headed for a match in Santiago, Chile. Tragically, the squad would not make it to their destination. At 3:30 p.m., as the players threw a rugby ball around the cabin of the plane, the aircraft crashed into the Andes Mountains. Nando recounts his experience, "There was a howl of metal grinding. . . . I saw the sky above me. Frigid air blasted my face, and I noticed with an odd calmness that clouds were swirling in the aisle . . . then I was torn from my seat with incredible force and hurled forward into the darkness and silence."

The next morning, Nando regained consciousness to a throbbing pain in his head, "a pounding so raw and ferocious it seemed a wild animal had been trapped inside [his] skull and was clawing desperately to get out." Nando described the cold as "a savage bone-crushing cold that scalded [his] skin like acid." Even worse than his throbbing head and the bitter cold was the realization that 18 of his best friends and teammates had died in the crash.

Being relentless is all about taking action.

Nando decided that he would do whatever was necessary to live. He worked diligently to prepare a makeshift shelter to help him and others brave the frigid temperatures and serve as a rudimentary hospital to nurse those who were injured and ill. For 16 days Nando forced his thoughts toward a constant assessment of life, health, and resources.

On the evening of the 17th day, another problem arose. As Nando and his teammates were huddled in the belly of the fuselage, trying to use body heat to survive another of the frigid evenings, an avalanche came down the mountain, burying everyone and everything, creating a certain tomb of snow for those who remained. Eight more of Nando's teammates passed away in the avalanche. Still, Nando refused to give up. He forced his mind to focus on what could immediately improve his current situation—to dig. After eight days of digging, huddling for warmth, and fighting for their lives, Nando and 18 of his teammates found their way out from under the mountain of snow. While despair and grief gripped and defined many of his teammates, Nando forced himself to remain *optimistic*. Nando refused to accept failure, even as imminent death stood directly in his path time and time again. He stayed focused on what it would take to survive, no matter the circumstance.

On a daily basis, he worked to control his mind to emphasize and execute the solutions needed to overcome each and every obstacle. With no food available in the frozen tundra and starvation approaching, Nando wrestled with the personal dilemma of using his perished teammates' flesh for sustenance. He refused to let his emotions overtake him, and he *focused* on using his mental capacity to avoid death. After 30 days, starvation became the most pressing issue. Nando's solution to the starvation problem was not a popular one; however, Nando was relentless, and in the end, everyone did eat.

After 62 grueling days on the mountain, Nando realized help wasn't coming and decided that the only way to survive was to rescue himself. Nando climbed in subzero temperatures across some of the highest and most unrelenting mountains in the world. His focus of "one inch at a time" sometimes required hours to move even one single inch. Unbelievably, after 10 straight days of "one inch" focus, a physically weakened Nando emerged out of the mountain wilderness after traversing more than 70 miles to safety. And he was able to direct rescuers to his 16 surviving teammates.

Nando's story is one of my favorites, and I often use it in speaking events as an introduction to what RSF looks like. Nando vowed he would never get trapped by his own expectations. There were times in his 72-day journey that he lost confidence that he would actually survive. In those moments of darkness, he realized the power and energy in maintaining a solution focus:

> I saw myself crawling, until my hands and knees were shredded. Finally, I fell to my belly and dragged myself with my elbows until my strength was gone. At that point, I assumed I would die. In my altered state of mind, these images did not distress me. In fact, I found them reassuring . . . There were things I could do. There would still be space between my death and me.

In those most critical moments Nando wasn't sure if he would actually survive, but he realized if he were to die, in his last days and hours, he wanted his mind focused on solutions. Giving in to his problems was actually more painful than death itself.

Nando's quest for survival obviously involved incredible amounts of the physical toughness that we might assume from an international rugby star. Yet the key to his survival and what set him apart from the others was his *mental* toughness.

Mental toughness saved Nando's life. I want you to realize that to be truly successful and fully satisfied with life, you need to learn to take the same relentless approach to developing your mental toughness. Your quest for happiness depends on it.

What are you aiming for? Are you aiming simply to survive your career? If you are constantly setting your sights as low as getting through the day and doing your job—the corporate equivalent of mere survival—are you really achieving the quality of life you want? Are you, like some of Nando's teammates, waiting to be saved by someone or something else? Most of us go through life waiting—waiting for the next big idea to strike us, waiting for the client to sign on the dotted line, waiting for the big promotion, waiting for the competition to run out of steam, waiting for the giant bonus, waiting for our spouse to change, or waiting for our kids to grow out of a difficult phase. Waiting is mental weakness. We wait patiently and politely, never realizing, as Nando did, the importance of deciding exactly what *we* need to do for ourselves and then pursuing those actions with relentless vigor.

Hearing the inspirational stories of others is like hearing a good pep talk. Don't get me wrong, I love a good pep talk; however, a pep talk doesn't change your life for long, and it won't win you a World Series, get you to the top of your profession, or boost and sustain your personal happiness. To reach your relentlessness potential, you need a proven game plan.

To truly develop the relentlessness skill, you must master the ability to recognize PCT and then replace it with solution-focused thinking using the RSF tool.

Relentless means that when you commit to something, you *never, ever* give up. No matter what, you always keep yourself in the fight. Always. Whether it's trying to reach your professional aspirations, your financial goals, your ideal fitness level, or your goal of developing happy healthy relationships—whatever that summit is, no matter how many times you fail, you must continue to kick, scratch, and claw your way toward the finish line. The RSF tool is your way to keep clawing. Each obstacle in your path, you find a way to go over, under, around, or through. No matter how many times you get knocked down or told, "No," you refuse to give in or give up. That's relentlessness. Remember, failure fades when quitting isn't an option.

> **Relentlessness:** when you commit to something, you never, ever give up

If you have a heart beating in your chest, if there is a breath of air in your lungs, you need to be searching for solutions. Relentlessness requires that you keep using the RSF tool, asking yourself, *"What is one thing I can do differently that could make this better?"* until you remain on the solution side of the board. Challenge yourself never to stay on the problem side of the mental chalkboard for longer than 60 seconds. That is relentlessness.

SELF-EVALUATION

Think of being relentless like a boxing match. Rarely does a fighter win by throwing just one punch. The best fighters are those who are prepared to consistently throw punches round after round.

How many punches do you typically throw at a problem before you give in to PCT? Take a moment and answer another tough question. On a scale of 1 to 10, how relentless are you?

No matter what your answer is, don't beat yourself up. Doing so does nothing to make you better. Instead, use the RSF tool and ask yourself, *"What is one thing I can do differently that could make (my relentlessness) better?"*

Learning about people like Mark McLean and Nando Parrado is important because it serves as proof that the human spirit is capable of relentlessness. Personally, I have become much more relentless because of my studies of remarkable human beings. At one point in my career, I realized that immersing myself in stories of people who exemplified how we as humans are capable of going beyond the way we are biologically wired had begun to rub off on me.

However, this is not enough. Remember, *knowing* something does nothing to change things; *doing* something does. By the time you finish this book, you will know exactly how to train yourself to be relentless—your mind will be ready to fight when adversity strikes.

③ THINGS TO *KNOW*

1. Relentless means that when you commit to something you *never, ever* give up. No matter what, you always keep yourself in the fight. Always. The only person who can take you out of the fight is you. You're never out of the fight unless you choose to be.
2. Your thoughts are *always* your choice. When you choose to believe that quitting isn't an option, failure fades.
3. The RSF tool (*What is one thing I can do that could make this better?*) is the key to *replacing* negative thoughts with solution-focused thinking, moving from the problem side to the solution side of your mental chalkboard.

① THING TO *DO*

Take a moment right now and create the mental chalkboard on a piece of paper, like you did at the end of Chapter 4. Draw a line vertically down the middle. Title the left column "Problem" and the right column "Solution." Write the RSF tool question somewhere on the paper to serve as a reminder for how to get from the problem side to the solution side.

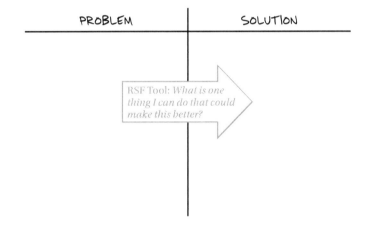

PROBLEM | SOLUTION

RSF Tool: *What is one thing I can do that could make this better?*

On your diagram, identify one problem you are currently experiencing in your life, and then with relentlessness ask yourself the question, *"What is one thing I can do that could make this better?"* to come up with a solution that puts you back in control and improves your current situation. Remember, even an inch of improvement counts. You may find that your first solution sticks, or you may have to ask the question several times until you come up with one that you don't cross off. Once you have a solution that sticks, fold your mental chalkboard and place it in a pocket, wallet, or purse, or hang it in a place as a visual reminder of your mental toughness. Make the commitment to yourself that no matter what, you will not give in to this problem. No matter how long it takes, you will continue to fight this problem to the very end. *Be relentless and stay in the fight.*

6

The Plus 1 Concept

Improvement over Perfection

David Goggins decided he was going to run a 100-mile race, and when David Goggins decides he is going to do something, he does it. Keep in mind David was already the first person in US military history to complete three of the US armed forces' most prestigious trainings: Navy SEAL training, US Army Ranger School, and US Air Force Tactical Controller Training. The only problem with running 100 miles in 24 hours was that David knew very little about what it would take to accomplish this feat, and he was ill-prepared to do so. He and his wife showed up on race day and came to the quick realization of just how underprepared he might be. He noticed the other racers all had "teams" of people for support. There were nutrition coaches, medical personnel, and strategy advisors. David's "team" consisted of his wife, and his "nutrition" included some Ritz crackers and a few bottles of PowerPlex.

Through pure will and desire, David completed 70 miles in roughly 13 hours. After doing so, he admittedly was "messed up badly." He sat down with his wife to evaluate his situation, but that only caused it to worsen. His muscles were seizing up to the point that he was unable to even stand up. He later found out that he had multiple stress fractures in his legs and feet, torn muscles, and severe shin splits. Needing to use the restroom that was a mere 20 feet away, David elected to relieve himself while sitting in his chair. With blood, urine, and feces running down his legs, finishing the race seemed impossible.

Then David Goggins did something that most people don't do. He didn't allow his mind to focus on the 30 miles he had left or the severity of his condition. Instead, he focused on *one thing*. He broke the 30 miles down into very small, bite-sized chunks that he could more easily digest. His first goal was to hydrate. He asked his wife for some water, and he focused on getting it down. Then he zeroed in on getting himself cleaned up. He wiped himself clean and found another pair of shorts. Nutrition was next. After having something to eat, his next goal was simply to stand up.

Once standing, David set his sights on taking one step. And then another, and another. It was a small victory every time he took one step. After 11 miles of "one step at a time," David's wife told him that he wasn't on pace to make the 24-hour deadline. He put compression tape on his feet, ankles, and shins so that he could run the last 19 miles, which he did "one step at a time."

By chunking the last 30 miles into small pieces, David Goggins was able to complete the race in time. He later said, "We have the ability to go to such a space, and if you are willing to suffer, your brain and your body once connected together can do anything."

The lesson in David's story—great successes are built on small victories. When a person learns to emphasize improvement over perfection, progress accelerates dramatically.

When a person learns to emphasize improvement over perfection, progress accelerates dramatically.

THE ENTIRETY PERSPECTIVE

When the human mind is presented with a new situation, the normal way of sizing it up is first to view it in its entirety. When we see a forest, we overlook the trees themselves. If you see a house, you don't take much notice of any one window or door, but rather the entire structure. This has do with *channel capacity*, the brain's biological bandwidth. Our minds have limited ability for attentional focus. We have only so much room in our brains when surveying our environment. When we see the big picture, we lack the ability to comprehend all the details making up that big picture in the same moment. If we zero in on the details of a single tree, then the forest itself begins to fade.

> **Entirety perspective:** when the human brain is presented with a new situation, the normal way of sizing it up is first to view it in its entirety
>
> **Channel capacity:** the brain's biological bandwidth

In many regards, focusing on the big picture first is very helpful for the human organism. Think back to prehistoric times. Not surveying the entire landscape, but focusing only on that one berry bush was a surefire way to end up in the lion's den. Unfortunately, seeing things through the entirety perspective oftentimes causes problems to appear insurmountable. As David Goggins experienced, the key to overcoming difficult problems is to chunk them into small pieces. We call this process "ask and chop." When faced with a daunting problem, simply *ask* yourself, "What is the first step in getting through this?" In doing so, you immediately *chop* any big problem into something much more manageable.

Less Is More

James, a client of mine, is a financial advisor. He is very good at what he does, and he is extremely passionate about helping his clients reach and exceed their financial goals. His desire to help his clients has at times been overwhelming for him. In a recent coaching session, I could immediately hear panic in James's voice. He was talking a mile a minute, "Jason, the markets are down over 30 percent, and right now, I need to get in touch with all of my clients and make sure they aren't freaking out, and for those who have extra money, now is the time to buy."

Now keep in mind, James has close to 400 clients. I wanted to know if he had created a game plan for identifying who should be called first, and specifically how he could effectively get through his entire client list. I asked James how many client contacts he had made in the previous workday. He responded, "I returned four calls and met with three people via WebEx. That took over five hours of my day. By the time I finished the paperwork for those calls and meetings, it was past 7:00 p.m., and I had to get home to my family." I calmly asked James, "Do you realize, at that pace, it will take you more than 57 days to get through all of your clients?" James responded with silence. His response told me what I needed to know. I then asked him one more question, "On a scale of 1 to 10, where is your confidence right now?" In a defeated tone he answered, "At best, I'm a 3."

Allowing yourself to believe that you must perfectly solve all of the problems that you or those in your life have is obviously a losing proposition. A perfect solution for every problem is not a reality, but that's not the point we want to underscore here. It's important to understand the impact of overloading your channel capacity.

The magic numbers to remember with channel capacity are *three* and *one*: Holding focus on no more than three items and learning or improving only one new concept at a time.

Trying to remember or hold focus on more than three items is extremely difficult to do with any consistency, especially over longer periods of time. And a person should not try to learn or improve more than one new concept at a time. Respecting channel capacity is similar to juggling. A person can typically juggle three balls, but when you throw a fourth one into the mix, a person usually drops multiple or even possibly all of those balls.

Think of it this way: your brain is like the photo album on your phone. When the memory capacity of the photo album fills, your phone lets you know and asks you to delete the photos you no longer want. When you overload the channel capacity of your brain, unfortunately, you don't get to choose what gets deleted (or forgotten). For most of us these days, our mental bandwidth is already overfilled and bursting at the seams. That is why it is so common for us to forget really important things and overlook really important details.

Overloading channel capacity levies a heavy toll on confidence. Trying to focus and execute on too many things at once is a total recipe for inconsistency, and inconsistency erodes confidence. If self-confidence is low in one area, it bleeds over into other areas. When individuals learn to focus and execute on one very important task, self-confidence rises, and other areas of performance improve as well.

---

*When individuals learn to focus and execute on
one very important task, self-confidence rises,
and other areas of performance improve as well.*

After giving James a quick review on channel capacity, I asked him another question, "On a scale of 1 to 10, how often are you identifying your most important activity daily and making certain to start the day by attacking it?" James answered bluntly,

"I'm not. I get to the office, and I start returning phone calls, putting fires out, and it seems like that lasts all day. I stopped writing down my most important daily activity three weeks ago, about the same time this whole coronavirus thing began. I know I need to be making 20 or so contacts daily, talking to my people about what to do. I honestly feel like 20 contacts isn't even possible, so I end up playing defense all day and not getting any of those proactive contacts made."

I asked James to make one simple adjustment, "For the next three days, I want you to get to the office on time, and before you do anything else, I want you to proactively call three clients. I don't care what else happens that day, as long as you make your three proactive calls in the first hour, you have won that day." James called me the next day in the late afternoon and said, "Jason, that was really helpful, thanks for the direction; but at this pace, it will still take me too long to get through all the calls." I asked James how long each of his three calls took on average. "By the time I get through everything I need to cover with them, each call is lasting 20 minutes or so." I gave James one more directive, "For each of those three proactive calls, I want you to decide on the one most important thing your client needs to hear right now, and that is all you can discuss on this round of calls." Notice that I was asking James to do *less*, not more.

I spoke to James three weeks later, and he had this to say:

> It took three weeks, but we got through every client—well, at least all the clients we felt needed to hear from us. I started the day with a goal of getting three calls made, but trimming down to only one item to discuss allowed me to get closer to 8 to 10 calls a day. I also realized my two assistants could help with the calls. Thinking about doing less undoubtedly gave me, or I should say us, the ability to do more.

Creating extensive to-do lists with a goal of getting everything done each day is a total mistake. Force yourself to identify your three *most important* and one *must* tasks daily. Before the end of each day, take a couple of minutes to identify your three most important to-dos for the next day, and of those, figure out which one task is most important and must get done first. Focusing on doing *less* is a great way to honor channel capacity and keep confidence and performance high.

Learned Helplessness

In 1970, researcher and psychologist Martin Seligman first coined the term *learned helplessness.* Seligman placed dogs in a box where electric shocks were administered. While this experiment certainly wouldn't pass institutional review board standards today, much was learned from it regarding human behavior. The dogs in the experiment could avoid being shocked by simply pressing a lever inside the box. The majority of dogs learned to press the lever and escape being shocked. A second group of dogs were placed in the same box where they received shocks. However, for this group of dogs, pressing the lever did not stop the electric current. The shocks happened no matter what the dogs did. Then Seligman removed this group of dogs and placed them in another box where pressing the lever *would* indeed stop the shocks. To his surprise, these dogs no longer even attempted to press the button to avoid being shocked. The dogs learned in the first exercise that there was nothing they could do to avoid the electric current, so they stopped trying. The dogs believed there was no hope and nothing they could do to control their environment. This is *learned helplessness.*

Learned helplessness doesn't just happen with dogs. Viewing life through the entirety perspective contributes to learned helplessness in humans. When people experience failure, they lose hope. When hope is removed, we give up and stop making future attempts at solutions. Essentially, most people give up without a fight if they become discouraged early in the solution process.

As pitiful as this sounds, it makes sense. People quit when they feel there is no point in trying. It's the equivalent of losing the game before even taking the field. When a person considers climbing a mountain, the initial thought is to look up to the summit and then begin assessing the possibility of making the full climb. Oftentimes, people become so consumed with the *potential* for failure or setbacks that they don't even open their minds to the possibility of succeeding. This is where learned helplessness sets in. A person lets himself experience multiple failures in his mind, causing him to quit without even taking the first step.

> **Learned helplessness:** when a person experiences failure—real or imagined—he loses hope and ceases trying

When is the last time you allowed yourself to experience learned helplessness by not forcing yourself to break a large problem down into smaller more overcomeable steps?

I vividly remember a Navy SEAL friend of mine, Bob Gassoff Jr., talking to me about how he has been able to persevere in seemingly impossible circumstances. He said that giving up just isn't a choice he makes. He would rather die than give up. Navy SEALs *need* to be relentless, or they do not make it through Basic Underwater Demolition/SEAL (BUD/S) training. BUD/S is 24 weeks of the most difficult mental and physical training known to man. It is not uncommon for SEAL candidates to get less than an hour of sleep daily while running the equivalent of a marathon each day, carrying the weight of a boat on their backs. Only the mentally toughest and physically strongest can survive such training.

While Bob was going through BUD/S, he was completing a weighted swim exercise in which he had to swim an unfathomable number of lengths of the pool with weights strapped to his body. Bob will admit he is not the strongest swimmer in the Navy, and he was really struggling to complete the challenge. He got to a point where he knew he wasn't going to finish. His only two options were to tap out or to continue to try. He knew full well that "continuing to try" would cause him to pass out, and the weights strapped to his body were going to drag him under the water. Refusing to quit, Bob chose to stay in the fight and focus on his next stroke. He passed out and began to sink to the bottom of the pool. Thankfully, instructors got to him before it was too late. What sticks with me to this day is that he made the choice to not give up, knowing full well the possible outcome. Of course, this is an extreme example of staying in the fight, but I hope you see the main point. You and you alone determine if you stay in the fight. One of the most powerful things I have learned in my studies of mental toughness is that some things are worse than death. Remember Nando Parrado's story from the last chapter? When he allowed his thoughts to focus on how bad his situation was, living became intolerable. In a very similar manner, Bob Gassoff Jr. has chosen to live life with the attack mentality. Never quitting, never giving in to the fight.

SEAL candidates know the most common time for quitting is during "chow time." The BUD/S instructors are ruthless when the candidates are eating. They know that's when they are most vulnerable to the psychological warfare of the entirety principle. That's when they begin to tell future SEALs what they can expect after they finish eating. "We will start with an eight-mile boat run, then move to two hours of surf training, and then when we are good and warmed up, we will run a few laps through the obstacle course, and that is just the first eight hours." The mentally weak allow their minds to become overwhelmed with *everything* that needs to get done—to a point where quitting seems to be the only option. The mentally strong refuse to look at the entirety of the day, but rather focus on the first step of that eight-mile run. Instead of being hopeless, they make themselves hopeful.

I later asked Bob how he could get through such a difficult process. He told me the only way he found to survive was to concentrate only on "one step." He forced his mind to blur out everything else, and he focused only on the very next step. Focusing on one step made staying in the fight easier, and it held thoughts of quitting at bay. One step at a time, step after step, Bob won the battle against giving up. Whether it was an eight-mile boat haul, three hours on the obstacle course, or two hours of surf training, he would narrow his focus and win the next step. Not only did Bob finish BUD/S training, he was one of the top in his class and has since risen to the rank of lieutenant commander.

Remember, all problems have solutions when broken down into small enough pieces. There is always a solution. Always. An integral aspect of successfully adopting an RSF mindset lies in knowing this. If you believe there could be a problem with no solution, sooner than later you will lose your battle against PCT.

THE PLUS 1 CONCEPT

The common definition for *solution* is "complete resolution." In other words, "perfection." This is a terrible definition because it causes people to view problems and solutions through the entirety perspective. A much more appropriate and productive way to define a solution is "any improvement whatsoever to the current situation." The smallest unit of measure—even one inch—of improvement counts. Even one inch of improvement *is* a solution. This is why we call this the *Plus 1 solution.*

> **Plus 1 solution:** any improvement whatsoever to the current situation

Stop trying to solve your problems in their entirety, and instead learn to chip away at them. You will be surprised at just how far you can get in life. Replacing problem-focused thoughts with Plus 1 solutions is the key to developing mental toughness and unlocking human potential, especially when our problems seem insurmountable. Unfortunately, this can be much more difficult than it sounds.

I developed the Plus 1 concept early in my career while working with a veteran Major League pitcher rehabbing from Tommy John surgery. Prior to the injury he was a dominant force on the mound. At well over six feet tall, he aggressively pounded the strike zone, carving up even the best hitters in the game. When the news came that he needed surgery, he called me to let me know he was going to retire because he didn't feel like he was up for a long year of rehab. He already had, by any account, a very successful career, and financially he was set for life. But I knew that even though he could retire with pride, he wasn't ready to leave the game. It was obvious he still loved playing. He was a respected teammate and a true leader.

I convinced him to put off announcing his retirement for one day. We spoke daily for a week, each time ending with the "wait one day" conversation. This went on for months. It actually became a joke between us, as he made very small steps of progress each day. A year later, with his rehab finished, he found himself pitching in what would turn out to be one of the best years of his career. He called me and thanked me for the support and belief saying, "That *one more day* idea really worked!"

The mere act of living on the solution side of the mental chalkboard causes a significant improvement in health, happiness, and success. Remember, this does not necessarily require finding perfection or complete resolution, rather just *searching* for solutions. These solutions become much easier to find when you are looking for only the very next step—any improvement to the current situation. Breaking a problem down into smaller, more manageable chunks makes it much easier to keep one's mind on executing solutions.

LEARNED HELPLESSNESS AND DECISION MAKING

Not chopping problems down into smaller, more manageable pieces ensures that you remain on the problem side of your mental chalkboard. Aside from the havoc living on the problem side of the mental chalkboard wreaks on your health, self-confidence, and happiness, the effects on decision making are a serious threat to success. When we don't allow ourselves to move forward one inch at a time, one Plus 1 solution at a time, we are at serious risk of moving significantly backward.

The longer we spend on the problem side of the board, the higher the cortisol levels, the more our negative arousal climbs. Think about the last you were ruminating on a problem. Whether you felt it or not (my guess is that you did feel it), your heart rate probably increased, your body temperature likely rose, and you might have gotten sweaty or even sick to your stomach.

This results in a negative emotional state that impairs your cognitive function (or mental ability). Decision making is a highly important aspect of cognitive function, and like it or not, if this is impaired, you are more likely to make dumb decisions. Think of it like a seesaw: the higher your emotional state, the lower your cognitive ability.

Not only do we know that arousal affects our decision making, research has also shown that people are generally bad at predicting just how much it will do so. In his book *Predictably Irrational,* Dan Ariely wrote about an experiment he conducted with his colleague George Loewenstein at Berkeley, in which they looked at the effect of arousal on decision making. They had college-age men complete surveys about the likelihood they would engage in unsafe or immoral behaviors. The participants answered the questions very differently when they were actually aroused versus when they weren't. When judging their propensity to engage in immoral behaviors, participants judged themselves more than twice as likely to engage in such behaviors when they were aroused than when they were in a "cold state." In a cold state, the participants were rational in their responses, and these responses reflected an avoidance of unsafe and immoral behaviors—generally a "moral high ground." The participants also grossly miscalculated what they would find themselves capable of when in a "hot state."

Basically, they thought they knew themselves, but they didn't. And by "they," I mean all of us. Ariely likens this to Jekyll and Hyde. No matter how good we think we are, when our irrational self takes hold, we are capable of things we wouldn't expect. This is why you may leave a store having spent way more money than you are comfortable with because you were wooed by the excitement of the moment, or why you may have responded with an uncharacteristically harsh jab in the middle of an argument.

These types of reactions are easy to brush off as getting "lost in the heat of the moment," but what about when we are making decisions after being lost on the problem side of the mental chalkboard? One of my favorite quotes by Edwin Louis Cole says it best: "You don't drown by falling in the water; you drown by staying there."

It is common for people to get so lost on the problem side that they remain inactive to *any* decision, but research tells us that the negative arousal associated with the stress and anxiety from swirling around on the problem side of the mental chalkboard may produce *bad* decisions that are counter to our self-identity. People have done horrible things after allowing a problem focus to take hold. Pull up any local or national news website, and many headlines provide proof of this. Most people doing bad things aren't actual "monsters," but rather normal people making very bad decisions because of PCT.

---

*"You don't drown by falling in the water;
you drown by staying there."*

Controlling your arousal state becomes much easier when a person chooses to focus on solutions. No matter how small the solution is, staying focused on it increases confidence and enhances performance. To control your emotions, you don't need to worry about solving a problem in its entirety. You just need to get out of the problem side of the mental chalkboard by using the RSF tool to come up with something that could result in any improvement whatsoever to your current situation (Plus 1 solution).

RSF is not about perfection, not about fixing the problem, but rather Plus 1 improvement. The good news is that the Plus 1 concept is built into the RSF tool. *"What is one thing I can do that could make this better?"* Sticking to the wording of the RSF tool makes it much easier for you to respect channel capacity and keep your focus on finding a Plus 1 solution within 60 seconds. Remember, when you encounter or catch yourself focusing on a problem, the key is to get out of the problem side and to the solution side of your mental chalkboard ideally within 60 seconds Identify one thing, just one step that begins to attack the problem, and you begin to form the habit of anchoring yourself in the RSF mindset.

Understanding that you only need to come up with something that could improve your situation by even one inch (Plus 1 solution) makes this much more manageable. If or when the first solution on the mental chalkboard is crossed off because it either didn't work or didn't result in resolution of the problem, you will likely find yourself back on the problem side. Get back to the solution side within 60 seconds by using the RSF tool to come up with another Plus 1 solution. Be relentless about this process until you can remain out of the problem side. As long as you don't allow yourself to stay on the problem side for more than 60 seconds, you are winning.

When our focus is on improvement (Plus 1 solutions), it frees our mind from the stress associated with perfection, allowing us to make much better decisions. Here are some examples of working through the mental chalkboard using Plus 1 solutions:

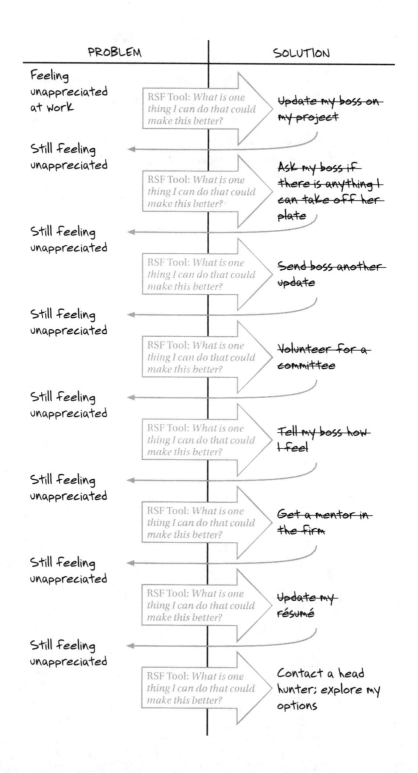

PROBLEM | SOLUTION

Feeling unappreciated at work

RSF Tool: *What is one thing I can do that could make this better?*

Update my boss on my project

Still feeling unappreciated

RSF Tool: *What is one thing I can do that could make this better?*

Ask my boss if there is anything I can take off her plate

Still feeling unappreciated

RSF Tool: *What is one thing I can do that could make this better?*

Send boss another update

Still feeling unappreciated

RSF Tool: *What is one thing I can do that could make this better?*

Volunteer for a committee

Still feeling unappreciated

RSF Tool: *What is one thing I can do that could make this better?*

Tell my boss how I feel

Still feeling unappreciated

RSF Tool: *What is one thing I can do that could make this better?*

Get a mentor in the firm

Still feeling unappreciated

RSF Tool: *What is one thing I can do that could make this better?*

Update my résumé

Still feeling unappreciated

RSF Tool: *What is one thing I can do that could make this better?*

Contact a head hunter; explore my options

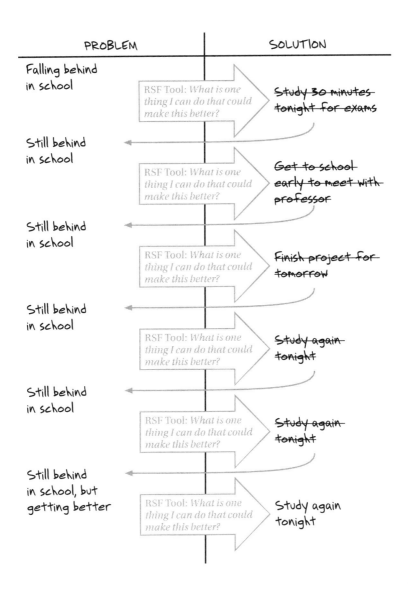

PROBLEM		SOLUTION
Falling behind in school	RSF Tool: *What is one thing I can do that could make this better?*	~~Study 30 minutes tonight for exams~~
Still behind in school	RSF Tool: *What is one thing I can do that could make this better?*	~~Get to school early to meet with professor~~
Still behind in school	RSF Tool: *What is one thing I can do that could make this better?*	~~Finish project for tomorrow~~
Still behind in school	RSF Tool: *What is one thing I can do that could make this better?*	~~Study again tonight~~
Still behind in school	RSF Tool: *What is one thing I can do that could make this better?*	~~Study again tonight~~
Still behind in school, but getting better	RSF Tool: *What is one thing I can do that could make this better?*	Study again tonight

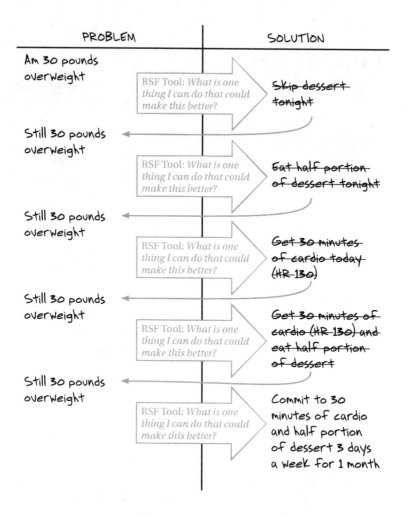

DON'T OVERCOACH

My good friend Tom Bartow once asked his best friend, the great coach John Wooden, what he thought was the biggest mistake coaches make. Coach Wooden quickly answered, "Tom, the biggest mistake coaches make is they overcoach."

Understanding the Plus 1 concept has changed the way Ellen and I coach our clients. The less advice we give, the better our clients perform. Let me explain. When I first started as a mental health professional fresh out of graduate school, I scheduled one-hour sessions with my clients. One hour was (and still is for most therapists and coaches) the standard, so I didn't even question it. Now, let me ask you, if you give a coach an hour, what is the likelihood that coach won't overcoach?

Respecting channel capacity and the Plus 1 approach forces me not to overcoach. Over the years, I gradually reduced my typical session time from 60 minutes to 45 minutes, and then to 30 minutes, and then finally, to no longer than 15 minutes. The key isn't to have longer meetings, but rather to be more relentless about identifying one and *only* one thing to improve.

With our clients, Ellen and I are focused on finding the next measure of improvement toward their goals, and once we identify that one step, we stop. What may seem slow at first is actually the fastest and most effective way to get there. Throwing technique after technique at people simply just isn't as effective as relying on the Plus 1 concept. The Plus 1 mentality makes focusing on what a person can control more doable. Instead of looking at problems or goals as overwhelming, people begin opening up to a whole new world of possibilities for positive outcomes, and they maintain the confidence to execute one solution at a time. Every year, our clients achieve greater and greater results in large part due to our improved ability to honor channel capacity.

REWIRING THE BRAIN

At this point, you have a pretty good understanding of the fundamentals of RSF and a solution-focused mentality. You may even be thinking, "Seems simple enough. I've got this." But remember, knowing something isn't enough. Very few people know how to actually *train* their minds for mental toughness.

Pep talks don't change biology. So far, this book has been nothing more than a pep talk, and even the best pep talk of all time won't overcome biology. If you want RSF to become your norm, you must train your mind for this change. Imagine this: You have two people of equal athletic ability. One person works out every day, and the other does nothing. This goes on for years, as one individual trains daily and keeps herself in tip-top shape, while the other does nothing. Let's say these two people were going to compete in a foot race. Who are you going to bet your money on? I know the one I am betting on, and I assure you my choice won't change even if the out-of-shape person is going to get a top-notch pep talk before the race.

To win at the highest level, you must train. The good news is that training the mind for RSF and mental toughness requires only three minutes per day. The more you train, the more mental toughness and the RSF mindset become your norm. You rewire the way your brain works.

You cannot (nor should you) prevent your brain from recognizing problems. We worry because we are advanced intelligent beings. The purpose of RSF is to replace problems with solutions much more quickly (within 60 seconds) than the brain is designed to do. With the right training, this not only becomes much easier, it also becomes your norm. Instead of countless hours of thought focused on what could go *wrong*, the RSF mindset emphasizes how life could go *right*. This frees up energy and mental capacity to live more fully and joyfully. If life does take a negative turn, the RSF mindset attacks problems quickly, without constantly waiting for the other shoe to drop. Simply put, those with the RSF mindset experience significantly less stress and more success.

Instead of countless hours of thought focused on what could go wrong, *the RSF mindset emphasizes how life could go* right.

To better develop the training strategy for mental toughness and the RSF mindset, you must understand the biology of the typical human brain and know what is necessary to change that biology.

Let's do a quick review of the important fundamentals up to this point:

1. **PCT:** Problem-centric thought is the biological tendency each of us has that makes it common to focus on problems or the negatives in life.
2. **Expectancy theory:** That which you focus on expands. The thoughts you choose to have directly impact how you feel and how you behave.
3. **RSF:** Relentless Solution Focus is the act of replacing all negative and problem-focused thinking with solution-focused thoughts within 60 seconds. The RSF tool and the Plus 1 concept are the keys to doing this.

It's true that PCT is hardwired into all of us, but we can actually rewire our brains with training. Neuroplasticity, the brain's ability to change neural pathways and synapses, makes possible the creation of new circuits that make being solution-focused the norm and PCT foreign. When it comes to the brain, there are two very important things to remember: neurons that fire together wire together, and neurons that fire apart wire apart. This theory was first introduced by psychologist Donald Hebb in 1949.

Through training, we can manipulate which circuits we want to reinforce.

The section of the brain we are going to work on starts with the *orbitofrontal cortex*. This area is located just behind our eyes. It's responsible for identifying problems and mistakes. When a problem or mistake is detected, the orbitofrontal cortex signals the *cingulate gyrus* that there is an issue. The cingulate gyrus, which is located in the deepest region of the cortex, initiates the experience of stress and anxiety. Working in cooperation with the cingulate gyrus is the *caudate nucleus*, located in the innermost center of the brain. The caudate is responsible for changing a person's focus from one thought to the next. Unfortunately, when the mind identifies a problem, it's normal for the caudate to be inefficient and allow more of a loop-type experience. The caudate has a tendency to get stuck in the problem, thus creating a "swirling effect" of problem focus.

Neurons that fire together wire together,
and neurons that fire apart wire apart.

When a person learns to break problems down into smaller steps (Plus 1 solutions), this makes it much easier for the caudate to release itself from getting "stuck" in the problem. With strategically targeted training, the caudate can be strengthened to allow a person to efficiently shift from a problem emphasis to solution-focused thoughts, which immediately releases the loop between the orbital cortex and the cingulate. We can train our minds, specifically the caudate, in as little as three minutes per day. Doing so creates new and more efficient mental circuits so that a person can move from a problem-filled world to a solution-rich life with ease and efficiency. As with anything else, the more you work on being solution-focused, the better you get at it, and the easier it becomes. When you train, you win.

Sound too good to be true? Well, it's not! Before you finish this book, you will know exactly what to do to begin retraining your mind to dramatically change your life for the better. Rest assured, it's not strenuous. It takes less than three minutes per day. We just need to formulate a game plan.

③ THINGS TO *KNOW*

1. The human brain is wired to initially size up problems in their entirety. This results in learned helplessness and people giving up hope without a fight.
2. All problems have solutions when broken down into small enough pieces. The focus should be on finding a Plus 1 solution to your problem.
3. A Plus 1 solution is defined as any improvement whatsoever to the current situation. Even an inch of improvement counts as a Plus 1 solution.

① THING TO *DO*

An integral part of RSF is getting to a place where you believe that *all* problems have solutions. It is easy to get wrapped up and overwhelmed when you are trying to solve problems in their entirety.

Draw another mental chalkboard, or use the one you created at the end of the previous chapter.

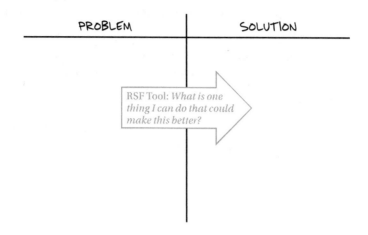

| PROBLEM | SOLUTION |

RSF Tool: *What is one thing I can do that could make this better?*

To continue your recognition and replacement of PCT, take the next 24 hours to focus on chopping your problems into manageable pieces by identifying Plus 1 solutions on your mental chalkboard. This is no different than the way we've already asked you to start using your mental chalkboard, but now you have a deeper understanding of what "counts" as a solution. For the next 24 hours, anytime you find yourself focusing on a problem, break the problem down by identifying a Plus 1 solution—identify one thing about the problem that you can improve. The goal is to find that first step or "one inch" of improvement. Of course, you won't always have a drawing of the mental chalkboard with you whenever you encounter a problem in life, but creating and using the visual now will help kickstart the process of recognizing and replacing PCT.

Learn to define "winning" as the ability to live on the solution side of the mental chalkboard. As you can see, RSF isn't going to solve your problems immediately. Instead, it keeps you in the fight. If you stay in the fight long enough—if you refuse to remain on the problem side—you will win. The key is to be *relentless* about finding that one inch—that Plus 1 solution.

PART III

RETRAIN

When You Train, You Win

7

The Framework
of Achievement

Vision + Integrity = Happiness

March 19, 2006, was my first day working for the St. Louis Cardinals. I can still remember going from field to field at the Jupiter, Florida, spring training complex. I was immediately impressed with the intensity and focus from the players and the coaches. It was clear that this was a world-class organization. These guys weren't out there just throwing balls around and slowly getting warmed up to play "real" games once the season began. Each of the 12 practice fields was filled with skilled athletes running through drills with precision. While one field of players ran through double play ball after double play ball, the next field had pitchers matched up against hitters. The players knew they were being evaluated, and their careers were on the line. Even in mid-March, it was "go time."

My role during spring training was to work individually with certain players who the organization felt would benefit from learning the tools and techniques for developing mental toughness. My day would begin with giving a large-group pre-sentation in the morning, and then throughout the afternoon and evening, I would have one-on-one sessions with players. No one in the organization told me how to do my job; however, there was a clear expectation that the players working with me would perform better than they had before. If I couldn't produce that outcome, I was told I would be fired immediately. For the entire six-year period I worked with the Cardinals, I never had a signed contract to guarantee my job. Thankfully, my players performed well, and I kept my position with the team.

I figured out exactly how much time I needed each morning with the team, as well as precisely how much one-on-one time I would need with each player. I would need to meet for 60 min-utes with eight players individually each day. I wanted to spend at least 15 minutes watching each player on the practice field before bringing him into the conference room to meet privately. In total, that would be two hours with the team, eight hours of individual meetings, plus another two hours watching players. I was already looking at 12 hours of meetings daily, and that didn't even include the time it would take me to find each player or to walk from each field back to the complex. Keep in mind, there are roughly 250 players practicing at any given time. I worried it would be somewhat like trying to find a needle in the haystack.

When I brought this dilemma to my boss, Walt Jocketty, he said that they could provide me with a golf cart and the master sched-ule indicating where each player would be every minute of each day. The St. Louis Cardinals had a strategic game plan for every player for every minute of spring training. Each player and coach knew *exactly* where to be and what he was supposed to work on for every minute of each day. It was abundantly clear that within all of this movement, there was a carefully thought-out game plan.

That year, the Cardinals won the World Series; they won another five years later in 2011. After the 2011 season, I stepped down as director of sport psychology to pursue some other opportunities, but I tell this story for this reason: If you want to position yourself to win the equivalent of the World Series in your life, you must—and I repeat, you *must*—have a strategic game plan, not just some general idea about improving. The same is true for training mental toughness and the RSF mindset.

HAVE A STRATEGIC GAME PLAN, NOT A GENERAL IDEA

The most successful organizations and individuals prioritize what is most important and deprioritize what is not. Highly successful people never get everything done on any given day, but they always get the most important things done each and every day.

For the RSF mindset to really take hold, there must be a strategy for training and execution. We need to specifically focus on strengthening certain parts of the brain (the caudate, in particular, which is responsible from changing a person's focus from one thought to the next) to more efficiently shift from a problem emphasis to solution-focused thoughts. To speed up the training, we don't want you to try to apply RSF to everything in your life. Otherwise, you will more than likely feel overwhelmed and fail at creating any consistent and long-term growth. Instead of trying to use RSF everywhere all the time with everything, we want you to have two specific activities for which you will commit to using RSF. Focusing on only two strategic areas lays a foundation for your mental toughness and in turn fuels your ability to have the RSF mindset in other areas of your life, as well.

Highly successful people never get everything done on any given day, but they always get the most important things done each and every day.

It is important that we do a bit of work before you determine what those two activities will be. We need to have a specific game plan, not just a general idea. If you walk away from this book thinking, "I'll just generally try to be more positive and solution-focused in my life," then Ellen and I have totally failed you. You won't get far without a few definite and measurable adjustments. Operating without a specific framework and precise game plan is a recipe for inconsistency and failure. The remainder of this chapter will help you strategically identify the two most important activities best for you to begin training and developing the RSF mindset.

Please trust me here. I have worked with people for more than 20 years developing the RSF mindset, and the two biggest mistakes I see people make are that they convince themselves they can overcome the problem-centric thought (PCT) biology without consistently completing the three minutes of training, and they try to apply RSF to all aspects of their life without first building a strong foundation of RSF on only two items. By identifying your two areas of focus, you will much more quickly and effectively be able to have the RSF mindset help you in all areas of your life.

Take your time working through the remainder of this chapter. The next few chapters are not meant to be a quick read. Chapters 7, 8, and 9 are more like a workbook. We would advise you to slow your pace for the rest of this book. Sometimes going slow is the fastest way, and this is one of those times. It's like building a house; if you cut corners and rush through putting in a solid foundation, it will certainly cost you in later phases of construction. Do the exercises we have outlined for you, and you will more quickly get to the final destination of having a solid foundation of mental toughness and RSF.

DEVELOPING THE FRAMEWORK: V + I = H

To best identify the two activities for you to begin applying RSF, we need to first figure out what is most important to you. The most effective method for doing this is by having you fill in some specific details within a consistently proven framework of success known as V + I = H. The "V" stands for vision, the "I" stands for integrity, and the "H" stands for happiness.

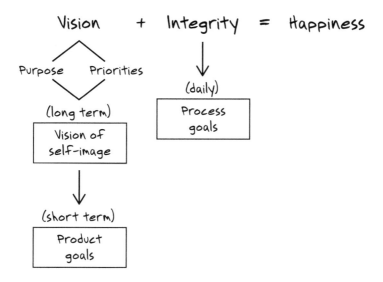

When you have a clear idea of where you want to go in life (vision), and you are confident that you are doing the most important activities on a daily basis to get there (integrity), there is no better formula I have found for reaching the ultimate level of success (happiness). It is difficult to sustain the daily grind required to achieve greatness if you don't have a clear idea of what you are working for. Without a framework, people flounder. They experience inconsistent results because they put in inconsistent effort. There is a great quote by Yogi Berra, "If you don't know where you are going, you'll end up someplace else."

Think about it. What pushes you through tough times or motivates you to keep going when you want to quit if you don't *really* know *why* you are doing it? I wouldn't recommend anyone put in significant effort toward something for no reason. That just doesn't make sense. So why do we allow ourselves to do this with our lives? In today's world, so many people live by the motto, "Busy is great," or "More is better." This is terrible, in my opinion. This is so bad for people's emotional states and for their performance. We have to know what is most important to us and why. Then and only then can we identify what it takes to get there and how to stay committed. As simple as this sounds, unfortunately, most people have not taken the time to figure out what they want, and specifically how to get it. Anything less than "what you want" isn't worth a significant investment of your time or energy.

Please answer the following two questions:

1. Do you know *specifically* who you want to be and how you want your life to look in five years?
2. Do you know *specifically* the two most important activities you must do daily if you are going to end up where you hope to be in five years?

If you had some idea of your answers to these two questions, but not necessarily the specifics, you are like most people. To give yourself a much-improved chance of getting what you want out of life, it is good to fill in the details. Never fear, in this chapter we will walk you through just how to fill in those most important particulars.

Prioritizing: The Most Underrated Skill

Rachel has always been an A-student in every sense of the phrase. In school, she finished every homework assignment on time (or early), completed every opportunity for extra credit (even though she didn't need it), was an accomplished college swimmer, and was always the one to get her group of friends together for dinners.

Rachel now runs an educational nonprofit organization, but she was finding herself consistently struggling to make payroll every month. Rachel is a go-getter, so she was always able to come up with some way to make ends meet, but she was getting worn down and exhausted by the constant uphill battle. Her marriage was struggling because she didn't have time to devote to it, and she was fighting burnout all the time. She had a lot of people counting on her for their livelihoods and for the organization's services, and the weight of that was starting to get to her. When Rachel came to me for help, the first thing we did was work to *prioritize*.

In my opinion, prioritizing is the most underrated skill of those who are most successful. These days most people get so caught up trying to get everything done that they compromise their ability to get the most important things done each day. Rachel was no exception. She was definitely putting more energy into getting *everything* done than she was attacking those more important tasks.

Prioritizing is the most underrated skill
of those who are most successful.

The goal was to simplify Rachel's life by zeroing in on those absolutely critical activities, while letting go of some not-so-critical items. She was a great example of someone who tries to focus on everything and loses the ability to execute on the most important things as a consequence. This tactic had worked for her growing up because life was easier then—she had fewer responsibilities and fewer people relying on her. But as she got older, her responsibilities increased, and the stakes got higher. That's when she began to flounder.

Being the A-student that Rachel is, she had already read several business and self-help books to help put her back in control of her life before she came to me. When I first brought up the need to prioritize, Rachel proudly said to me, "I've already started saying 'No' to things that do not directly relate to one of my top priorities." She went on to say, "There are just so many things that I have going on that are important that I can't give up."

Everyone thinks he or she is the exception to the rule to prioritize. Most people think they simply have too many responsibilities to simplify and focus on the most important ones. Let's be clear. At first, prioritizing is very difficult. However, once a person begins down this road, the benefits become sharply noticeable. Rachel was trying to get everything done, and as a result, she was not getting the most important things done each day. She had a general idea of the most important things in her life, and she was able to justify most things that came her way as being "too important to not do."

Rachel was the opposite of lazy. It was hard for her to wrap her head around the need to focus on *less* because she had always been praised for doing *more*. She needed a specific game plan, not just a general idea. Unfortunately, most of us are like Rachel; we have never been taught how to improve and execute on the ability to prioritize in life.

Establishing Vision

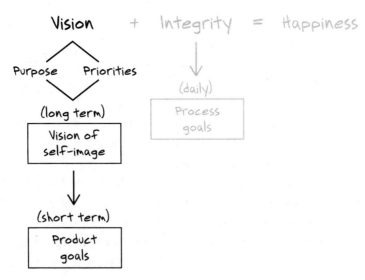

The first step to prioritizing and developing your game plan is to establish a vision. People like to skip this piece because it seems too big to grasp. If you don't know where you want to go, you have close to a zero percent chance of getting there, so let's figure out where you want to go. The two aspects of vision include where you want to go in the *long term*, and where you want to go in the *short term*. It is most impactful to think of long-term vision in terms of 3 to 10 years down the road, and short-term vision in terms of 12 months or less down the road.

To get us to your long-term vision, let's first ponder some big questions: What do you feel is your *purpose* in life? And what is most important to you (*priorities*)? Only from your purpose and priorities can you truly grasp your vision of how you want your life to be.

Purpose

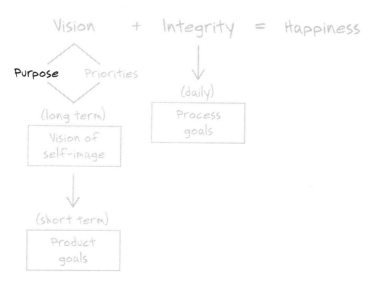

What is your purpose in life? Most people have not come up with an answer to this simply because it is such a big question. The key is not to worry about giving a perfect answer. Come up with something; you can always improve on it later.

My purpose in life is *to experience love and to help others.* Many of my clients try to come up with a purpose that is totally centered on others. While this is noble, it is important to have some aspect of your purpose in life that is centered on yourself and what brings you happiness. For example, "helping others" is the part of my purpose that is centered on others. It is certainly a big part of my life and is extremely important to me. Just as important is my need to "experience love." For me, this is a reminder that I need to allow myself to feel the love and appreciation from my friends, family, and clients, as well as to pursue the happiness and joy that life has to offer.

I know many people reading this will fight me on this and think, "Serving others is what makes me happy." For the thousands of people I have helped identify their purpose, I have not worked with a single person for whom it worked out to have a purpose that was 100 percent focused only on serving others. I am professionally advising you to identify your purpose with at least *some* aspect of serving yourself.

Consider Mother Teresa, one of the most selfless individuals to walk the planet. It is hard to find an example of a more selfless and loving individual, yet she was largely unhappy. I don't think that is fair. If anyone should be happy, it seems those individuals who devote their lives to others should experience great joy. Unfortunately, that is not necessarily the case. As with most things in life, there should be a *balance* of focusing on others, while also giving yourself permission to be a little selfish. I want you to find and maintain that balance.

Your purpose is your North Star. When you get off track, your purpose helps you remember why you do what you do, and it helps you determine if your actions are in line with your big picture. I will never forget a moment 15 years ago, when I was walking outside my front door to get the mail. My family was about to sit down for dinner as I walked to the mailbox, and I was incredibly preoccupied because I was waiting for a phone call about a big deal I was working on for a large corporate coaching job.

I remember walking toward the mailbox and having the sobering realization that I wasn't happy. I was waiting for confirmation of an incredibly big opportunity for my career, my family was waiting for me, and I had every reason in the world to be happy, but I wasn't. I realized in that moment that I had gotten so wrapped up in the money aspect of my career that it was creating a lot of stress in my life. This was one of those times when I had let myself get too focused on myself. I was being too selfish, and I was veering off track. My purpose got me back on track. I reminded myself that a huge part of my purpose was *helping others,* and part of that responsibility for me centers on being there for my clients, as well as my wife and children. If I stayed focused on that, the money would come. Once I got my mind right about why I was doing what I was doing, the pressure and stress lifted.

When you get off track, your purpose helps you remember why you do what you do, and it helps you determine if your actions are in line with your big picture.

Life can get complicated. Your purpose serves to simplify it for you. In a moment, we will ask you to write down your purpose. Albert Einstein said that "the definition of genius is taking the complex and making it simple." In my experience, simplicity is the key to success, and I have never seen an exception to this. So many people try to complicate success—do more, be busier. This mentality just does not yield sustainable results or happy people. The best coaches and the best teams focus on the fundamentals. Your game plan should be simple and precise. What are your fundamentals? The key is to identify what is important and then work to become really good at that.

Rachel determined that her purpose in life was *to have meaningful, loving relationships and to make a significant impact on her community.* Here are a few more examples of purpose from my other clients:

- To achieve greatness (corporate attorney)
- To live each day with patience, contentment, and generosity (CEO of a major pharmaceutical company)
- To experience love and push others to achieve excellence physically, mentally, and emotionally (gym owner)
- To make the world and myself better every day (professional football player)

There is no right answer when it comes to purpose. The only wrong answer is not to have one. It is important that you decide what your purpose is so you have a guiding light for how you live your life.

Take a moment now and do a quick rough draft on your purpose.

My purpose: _____

_____

Priorities

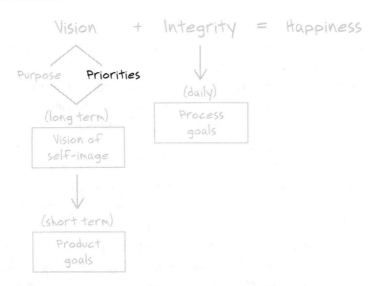

The next step in prioritizing is determining what is *most* important to you. Consider what your top three priorities in life are. There may be more than three aspects of your life that are important to you, but when you focus on the multitude, you lose the ability to succeed at the *most* important. Most of the people we work with identify priorities centered on *career success, relationship success,* and *personal health/happiness.* These are three themes that come up often, but your priorities do not have to match these. Trust your own instincts as to what is important to you in your life. There is no wrong answer (other than to not have an answer). Remember, if you don't know where you want to go, you have a very small chance of getting there. We want you to write these down again formally at the end of the chapter, but for right now take a quick shot at identifying and writing down your top three.

My top three priorities are:

1. _____

2. _____

3. _____

Rachel determined that her top three priorities in life were her *family* (she has a husband and a young daughter), her *relationships with her friends,* and her *career.* Rachel was on the right track to establishing her game plan, but she needed to do more work to make it specific. Without this next step, she was at risk of continuing to allow everything that came her way to fall into one of her priorities, and consequently, not devote the necessary amount of energy to what truly mattered to her.

Long-Term Vision: Vision of Self-Image

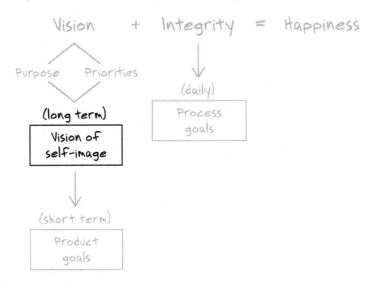

The next step is to determine a long-term vision through what I call a vision of self-image. Your vision of self-image is a detailed snapshot of who you want to be and what you want your life to look like 3 to 10 years down the road. For most people, looking beyond three to five years is very difficult. The research suggests that less than three years for this exercise might be too short of a time period, and longer than 10 years is probably too far away to be impactful. Most people settle on somewhere around five years from now, but trust your instincts on what time frame between 3 and 10 years makes the most sense for you. With your vision of self-image, it is OK to dream big. In fact it's advisable to do just that. It can open your mind to possibilities that you might not otherwise have considered.

> **Vision of self-image:** a detailed snapshot of who you want to be and what you want your life to look like 3 to 10 years down the road

Your vision of self-image should include details that represent where you want to be, based on your purpose and priorities. It's not about creating a vision with *everything* that you want in your life, rather focusing your purpose on the three priorities that are *most* important to you.

Rachel developed her vision of self-image for three years down the road, centered on her purpose in life *to have meaningful, loving relationships and to make a significant impact on her community*; and her top three priorities being her *family*, her *relationships with her friends*, and her *career*.

Rachel's vision of self-image:

My vision starts in the morning as I walk into my daughter's room to get her up for the day. I see her in her "big girl bed" peacefully sleeping in her room in our new house. There are still a few boxes left to unpack in her closet, but I take in all the toys and books strewn around her floor. I smile because I know she was excited to sneak in a little more reading time before she fell asleep the night before. I give her a kiss on the forehead and relish in the fact that I was able to wake up and enjoy a cup of coffee free from emails and work with my husband before we got going on our days. I didn't feel stressed about getting into the office because I was confident that things were organized for my arrival later in the morning. My daughter's eyes open, and a huge smile radiates across her face as she sees me. I love that we have created a home and environment for her that allows her to feel peaceful and secure. She sits up to give me the best hug in the world, and she jumps out of bed excited to start putting her toys away in her new room.

I see myself arriving at my lunch meeting with a potential high-level donor. I pull up to the restaurant 10 minutes early so I am able to casually get a table without feeling rushed or stressed. I sit down and open my email on my phone while I am waiting for her. I see an email that reads "Congratulations" on the subject line, and I know that means the organization received the $250,000 grant that I had applied for earlier in the year. I smile with satisfaction that the time I had put into the writing and the strategic plan had paid off. Once the potential donor arrives, I feel completely free of anxiety as I confidently convey my passion and plan for the organization. The donor tells me that she has heard wonderful things about our mission and execution from her "circle" of others of our high-level donors, and she was excited to be meeting with me. The meeting ends with her handing me a check and telling me that she can't wait to continue her involvement with the organization.

My vision then shifts to seeing myself at happy hour later that evening with my three best friends. We are laughing together and sharing stories about our kids over great wine. I see that we have remained close over the years in the midst of our families and careers, and we start making plans for a trip to Napa later in the year. I am excited about the trip, and know I have people and plans in place to allow the organization to be fine without me for a few days. I arrive back at home and relish in the fact that we have finally afforded our dream house in a great school district for our daughter. As I pull up, I smell the grill and hear my husband and daughter playing in the backyard. I put my phone away in my purse and place both my purse and computer away in the mudroom for the evening. I walk back to the yard to meet my family.

When Rachel wrote this vision of self-image, her mornings usually consisted of grabbing her daughter out of her crib and throwing her in her car seat quickly enough to get her to day care before Rachel ran into her first morning meeting (usually incredibly frazzled and a few minutes late). There always seemed to be something that would interrupt her schedule and put a wrench in her day. If she was lucky, she would get to spend a few minutes in the evening on the couch next to her husband before he went to bed, and she then would go through a mountain of emails on her laptop until midnight or later. She was surviving, and her organization was surviving, but that was not sustainable. She needed a clear game plan to get her life to a place where she was actually thriving. For the first time, Rachel's vision gave her clarity on specifically what she actually wanted her life to be.

Rachel wanted to feel connected to her friends and her family. She represented this in her vision of self-image by including peaceful and meaningful interactions with her daughter and her husband, and a relaxed and fun happy hour with her friends. She wanted to be in a stable and accomplished place with her organization. She represented this by including a congratulatory email about a grant and a big check from a new donor. She wanted to feel like she was running her life and priorities, not allowing external circumstances and overcommitments to run her. This was symbolized with a relaxed morning coffee date with her husband and by putting her phone and computer away for the night when she got home from work.

Constructing a vision of self-image gives you a clear picture of where you want to go so that you can start prioritizing what it is going to take to get there. Your vision of self-image is your "why." It's your dream life, and having clarity about what you want can be extremely motivating. Again, a general idea yields a general plan that likely results in spending too much time on what won't get you closer to where you want to be. Given that you have a finite amount of time and energy, by default, that means you are not spending *enough* time on what gets you where you want to be.

Take a moment now and jot down a few details for your vision of self-image. We will ask you to think about it again at the end of this chapter, but for now, just begin thinking about what it will entail:

Where do you want to live 3 to 10 years from now? Describe the home you envision. What city and state is it in?

_____

_____

_____

Where do you want to be financially?

_____

_____

_____

Who are the most important people you want to be a part of your life?

_____

_____

_____

What are the most important things you want to have accomplished?

_____

_____

_____

What is the state of your (physical, mental, and emotional) health?

_____

_____

_____

Short-Term Vision: Product Goals

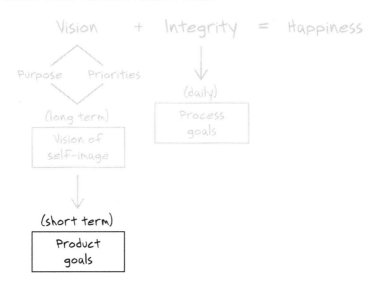

Now that you've done some thinking on your long-term vision, it's time to establish your short-term vision. This comes in the form of what I call *product goals*. A product goal is a *result-oriented goal attainable within 12 months*. These are likely the standard types of goals that you think of when you are goal-setting. For example, *I want to make a certain amount of money this year*, or *I want to lose a certain amount of weight by Christmas*, or *I want to have a better relationship with my spouse*. All of these are result-oriented goals.

> **Product goal:** a result-oriented goal attainable within 12 months

I want to be very clear that while it is OK to dream big when thinking about the long-term vision (3 to 10 years in the future), your short-term product goals (within 12 months) should be more realistic. The number one most common mistake that I see in goal-setting is the set-it-high-hope-to-get-close mentality. This method of goal-setting is only effective in time periods of three years or longer. Applying this mentality to goals for a time period of less than three years is highly ineffective because of its effect on self-confidence. Not to mention, it creates a habit of losing.

Think about it: let's say you set the goal of increasing your yearly revenue from $60,000 ($5,000/month) to $120,000 ($10,000/month) over the next year. In the back of your mind, you may know you will not hit that goal, but you put in the extra effort to get your revenue higher than it would have been otherwise. So for the first month, you get into the office early, stay late, make targeted phone calls, and you bring your revenue up from $5,000 to $7,500. That is a 50 percent increase and nothing to scoff at, but you are still 50 percent behind your goal for the month. That means you have to cover those losses in the following months.

During the second month, you continue your increased effort and bring in $8,000. You are now $4,500 behind where you should be for the first two months to hit your $120,000 goal for the year, but still well ahead of where you were last year. Remember, you told yourself you wanted to hit $10,000 per month, and now you've failed at it two months in a row. You should be feeling great about your improvement, but instead, you are beginning to beat yourself up for being behind.

In month three, you bring in $6,500 and dig yourself deeper into the hole. Because you are consistently missing your unrealistically high target, you are consistently learning that you don't hit your goals, and you don't achieve what you say you will achieve. You are forming the habit of losing. The effect this has on a person's self-confidence is incredibly detrimental and significant for performance. Most people would not continue to put in the effort beyond the first couple of months toward a target that they consistently miss—if they even make it that far. This is why most people don't have goals six months into the year, and most give up on their goals well before that. This is an incredibly common mentality and incredibly ineffective.

A good marker for setting realistically high product goals is a 10 to 20 percent increase. I have found that setting realistically high goals gives you a better chance of blowing through them and having that big breakout year; however, setting them high and hoping to get close decreases the chances of achieving consistent 10 to 20 percent growth. Think of it this way, would you be happy if for the rest of your career you posted minimum gains each year of 10 to 20 percent?

The second most common mistake people make when setting goals is that they set way too many. Channel capacity tells us that our biology allows us to focus successfully on only a limited number of things at a time. Trying to "beat" this and do too much is a recipe for inconsistency. Rachel, the A-student that she is, was always trying to "do more" to "be better." Not only was she unsuccessful, she was miserable. The "busy is good, do more" mentality is so bad for performance and for emotional states. Remember, *happiness* is the goal, and you must define that on your own terms. When you narrow your focus to less, you make it significantly more likely that you will achieve more of what is most important to you.

Consider that you are driving your car, listening to the radio, and talking on the phone. You may get to the destination, but I guarantee that you did not do any of those things at 100 percent. Multitasking is a very bad idea for performance. Yes, it is possible to do several things at once, but it is impossible to do several things *to your potential* at once. You achieve better performance when you narrow your focus, rather than widen it. For this reason, we want you to narrow your focus to only two product goals: one personal and one professional. Forcing yourself to identify the two product goals that are most important increases the likelihood of achieving more. Doing so has a major impact on self-confidence, and you learn the habit of winning when it comes to goal-setting.

_____

*Focus on less, and achieve more of
what is most important to you.*

_____

Rachel set a personal product goal of *increasing her connectedness to her husband from a 6 to an 8 on a 10-point scale within the next 12 months.* In addition, she set a professional product goal of *increasing revenue from $500,000 to $600,000 through individual donors, grants, and corporate donations in the next year.* Setting both a personal and a professional product goal is important because finding success in one area while sacrificing the other is not the recipe for a happy life. Before Rachel started with me, she had been consistently sacrificing her personal life to keep her professional life afloat. As a consequence, she was disconnected from her friends and family, and her organization was merely surviving. When one area of your life suffers, oftentimes that spills over into other areas. You may think that you need to sacrifice a priority area of your life in order to save another one, but realize that if you work on prioritizing, you can have happiness across the most important areas of your life.

Here are a few more examples of personal and professional product goals.

Personal product goals:
- Lose 10 pounds by Christmas
- Be the best father I can be (go from a 7.5 to a 9 on a 10-point scale by my son's birthday)
- Run a marathon in the next year

Professional product goals:

- Make it to the top 10 percent in my firm next year
- Increase my client satisfaction score by 20 percent by December
- Open 100 new accounts in the next year

Take a moment right now and take a first pass at identifying one professional product goal and one personal product goal you want to achieve in the next 12 months. To help narrow it down, what is the single most exciting goal you want to achieve professionally and the single most important thing you hope to achieve in your personal life in the upcoming year? Be sure your product goals are completely measurable. Instead of saying, "Bring in more revenue this year," indicate exactly how much. Instead of saying, "Lose weight," assign a number to this. If your goal does not have a predetermined measure, do a self-assessment of where you are currently on a 10-point scale, and then determine where you'd like to be within 12 months. For example, if you want to be a better spouse, give yourself a score on a scale of 1 to 10, based on where you feel you are now and where you want to be within the next 12 months. For example, "Be the best spouse I can be—go from an 8 to a 9 by our next wedding anniversary." Please take a moment now to write down one personal and one professional product goal.

Professional product goal: _____

_____

Personal product goal: _____

_____

Integrity: Attack the Process

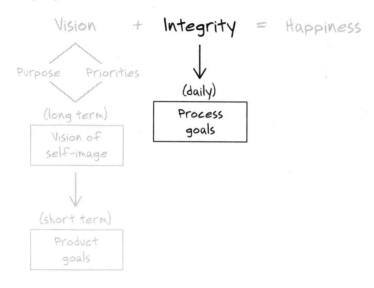

The third most common mistake people make when setting goals is what I call the paradox of the product goal: the more you focus on the product (result), the further you are from achieving it. While it is essential to know what results you are trying to achieve, the most successful have learned to put the majority of their effort and focus on the *process* that makes those results a reality.

When you learn to keep your focus on the daily activities required to achieve the result, the results begin to take care of themselves. Science tells us that the brain can fully focus on only one thing at a time. If you are focused on the result, by default, you are not focused on what you need to be *doing* to achieve it. We established the vision (vision of self-image and 12-month product goals) so that you know where you want to go. Now let's turn to the integrity portion of the framework (i.e., the process)—and fight relentlessly to keep our focus on the process.

The process focus was popularized by Coach John Wooden. When my good friend Tom Bartow asked Coach Wooden what he was focused on during a game, Coach Wooden quickly replied, "Tom, I am watching to see if my guys are running their cuts in straight lines instead of making their cuts in banana patterns." The greatest coach of all time wasn't looking at the scoreboard. He wasn't even concerned with the score, because he knew that if his guys were making cuts in straight lines instead of banana patterns, they would be faster than the other team. If his team was faster, the score would take care of itself.

These days in the sports world, you won't hear any great coach or great athlete talk about their success without talking about "the process." It was Coach Wooden who first showed the positive impact process can have on performance and winning, and now people are beginning to realize the positive impact it can have in the business world and in their personal lives.

What is the single most important daily activity for achieving your personal product goal and the single most important daily activity for achieving your professional product goal? These daily activities are your *process goals.*

Process goals: the most important daily activities required to achieve your product goals

For Rachel, the single most important daily activity that would put her in the best position to achieve her personal product goal (*increase her connectedness with her husband from a 6 to a 8*) was to *put her computer away by 9 p.m. every evening.* This may not seem like a huge commitment, but at the time, Rachel was regularly on her laptop until 11 p.m. or even midnight. Putting her computer away by 9 p.m. would give her an uninterrupted hour with her husband every night before bed, and as a bonus, would allow her to get to bed earlier herself. This was a *realistic* commitment that could make a significant difference in their relationship if she would commit to it. The single most important daily activity (process goal) that would put Rachel in the position to achieve her professional product goal (*increase revenue from $500,000 to $600,000*) was to *call two current or potential high-level donors daily.*

Her two process goals (computer away by 9 p.m. and two calls with current/potential donors per day) became her most prioritized activities because they were most integral to getting her to where she wanted to go. She told me that before she established these two process goals, she spent so much time doing many things that were "urgent" to the success of her organization, but would often allow meetings with donors to go unscheduled. Meeting face-to-face with donors was the most important activity to bring in substantial donations, but she realized that she was spending most of her time on less important tasks. Reaching out to those individuals daily was the most effective way of getting those face-to-face meetings.

Here are some examples of process goals for the product goal examples given earlier:

Personal Examples

- Product goal: lose 10 pounds by Christmas
  Process goal: do 30 minutes of cardio 5x week
- Product goal: be the best father I can be (go from a 7.5 to a 9 on a 10-point scale by my son's birthday)
  Process goal: spend 15 minutes of face-to-face time with my son each night, without the distractions of phone or TV
- Product goal: run a marathon in the next year
  Process goal: go on 3-mile runs 4x week; 6-mile run 1x week

Professional Examples

- Product goal: make it to the top 10 percent in my firm next year
    Process goal: spend 30 minutes each day preparing for presentations
- Product goal: increase my Client Satisfaction score by 20 percent by December
    Process goal: respond to all client emails within 24 hours
- Product goal: open 100 new accounts in the next year
    Process goal: make three proactive calls by 9 am every day

Take a moment now to rewrite your professional and personal product goals and determine a process goal for each (the *most* important daily activity required to achieve the product goal). These two process goals will become integrally important to you developing an RSF mentality and achieving your vision.

Professional product goal (page 151): _____

_____

Process goal: _____

_____

Personal product goal (page 151): _____

_____

Process goal: _____

_____

One of my all-time favorite quotes by Stephen Covey is, "The noise of the urgent creates the illusion of importance." Notice the word choice. Covey says it's an *illusion* that we fall prey to. I am not sure if you have ever seen an illusionist or not, but I have. A number of years ago I saw the Las Vegas act *Siegfried and Roy*. During the show, I remember thinking that I could not believe how real the magic appeared. It absolutely looked as though they were cutting a girl in half. Even though it seemed as though this young lady was being sawed in two, not one person in the theater called 911 or rushed the stage to protect her because we all knew that it was an illusion. I have found that when it comes to those urgent tasks that tempt you away from completing your process goals, you must remind yourself that they are nothing more than an illusion. Those tasks are not nearly as critical to your success as the "most important" activities—your process goals. When you establish those process goals, you must remind yourself they are the most important tasks that you need to absolutely get done each and every day. The urgency of any other task is just an illusion.

Once Rachel committed to getting her most important activities done before any of the other urgent daily tasks, she started seeing results in her organization's bottom line, her mental state, and her relationships. She became relentless about getting her two process goals done daily, and in doing so, her confidence began to soar.

Again, one of the biggest mistakes that is easy for people to make is to try to set way too many goals. Narrowing your focus and prioritizing your single most important task personally and professionally allows you to be much more successful at controlling the results. It may feel uncomfortable at first to commit to only two process goals (one personal and one professional), especially if you are currently overcommitted, but prioritizing your top two will make you significantly more successful.

③ THINGS TO *KNOW*

1. Most people either have no game plan or a very general one at best. Being specific increases success.
2. The three biggest goal-setting mistakes are: setting it high and hoping to get close, setting way too many goals, and focusing on the results instead of the most important daily activities (paradox of the product goal).
3. Become relentless about executing on your two process goals, and you will be much more successful at making meaningful and consistent change in other areas of your life. If you try to apply the RSF mindset to all areas of your life at once, you will likely feel too overwhelmed to sustain any progress.

① THING TO *DO*

It's time to document your game plan all in one place. On the next page, rewrite your purpose in life, your top three priorities, a personal and professional product goal, a process goal for each of these and construct your vision of self-image. Feel free to look back on your answers from earlier in the chapter; we included the page number to make it easier for you. You may be thinking that you already have these written throughout the chapter, so rewriting them is redundant. Let us assure you that the repetition of writing these details down is incredibly important. These are the details of your game plan, and rewriting them all in one place below will reinforce the importance of executing that game plan. Remember, this does not need to be perfect. Coming up with any answer that you can refine and modify as you go is miles ahead of coming up with no answer because you are afraid of choosing wrong. In this case, "done is better than perfect."

My purpose (page 140): _____

_____

_____

My top three priorities (page 141):

1. _____

2. _____

3. _____

Vision of self-image (use the details on page 146):

_____

_____

_____

_____

_____

_____

_____

_____

_____

_____

_____

_____

_____

_____

_____

_____

_____

_____

_____

_____

_____

_____

_____

_____

Professional product goal (page 155): _____

_____

Process goal: _____

_____

Personal product goal: _____

_____

Process goal: _____

_____

8

Perfection to Performance

Stop the Self-Inflicted Beatings

A number of years ago, one of the top kickers in the history of the NFL called my cell phone. When I answered the phone, I thought it was a prank. Keep in mind, I grew up with a group of guys who were practical jokers. Over the years, it has not been uncommon for a high school or college buddy to call me from an unrecognizable number and pretend to be someone else requesting my services. I have had fake calls from Gandhi, Mother Teresa, numerous presidents, famous actors, musicians, and authors. It is usually quite funny; however, in this case, when the player called, I embarrassingly thought it was a friend of mine doing another impersonation. After about 60 seconds, I realized it was indeed the great NFL kicker. I quickly apologized for not taking him more seriously and explained my initial unprofessional behavior. I then inquired, "You are already one of the best kickers in the history of the NFL. What in the world are you hoping I can help with?"

He responded by saying that he did everything he could possibly think to do each day in preparation to help his team on Sundays, only to find himself lying awake every night, filled with anxiety and stress, wondering if he had done everything possible to be fully prepared. It quickly became obvious that this guy had become such a success because of how much he cared. He was killing himself day after day in practice, and when he would get home at night, his mind would race, wondering if he had done enough. He was constantly second-guessing himself and searching to find ways to do more with his preparation. He wasn't actually calling me for help to become more successful at putting the ball through the uprights, but he needed help with his fear of not living up to the expectation of perfection that he had placed on himself over the years.

For the kicker, the perfectionist mentality began innocently enough when he was in high school. Because of his innate athletic ability, he was immediately a standout. Even in high school, his teammates and coaches realized he was special. He was the talk of the team during practices and games. Ever so slowly, he began to develop a perfectionist mentality—anytime he did something well, he would downplay it and write it off as "that is just what I expect of myself." Anytime he came up short, he would beat himself up about it. This seemed to him to be the best way to evaluate himself if he were to stay humble and hungry. At the high-school level of competition, his perfectionist mentality worked, but the only reason it did was because he had so many people telling him how great he was all the time. As he moved up in levels of competition, those external "pats on the back" would become more and more scarce.

Before the end of his junior year in high school, college offers were streaming in. After a strong senior year, he went off to college to play football on a full scholarship. In college, he would do plenty of things right in any given practice, but if one thing was done less than perfectly, he would focus only on the "less than perfect." He also noticed that he received fewer external pats on the back. Even though he was establishing himself as one of the top kickers in college, his teammates at this level were all standouts from their respective high schools. Being great was the standard at this level, and it was becoming increasingly difficult for him to feel good about himself and his performance.

Having done so well in college, he was drafted and earned a spot in the NFL. At this level, every player is among the best in the world. Pats on the back were few and far between. By this point, he had fully developed the perfectionist mentality: every time he did something well, he quickly overlooked it, and his mind focused only on his imperfections. Even though he was playing well at the highest level of competition, he wasn't happy. From the outside, it looked as though he had it all. He had a great well-paying job and a wonderful family, but on the inside his confidence was shot. By the time he called me, he was constantly anxious and stressed, never able to live up to the standard of perfection that he had set for himself. Something had to give.

The first assignment I gave him was to write down on paper exactly what he felt he needed to do in preparation each day leading up to game day. Each time he began to itemize what a complete day of prep looked like, he would second-guess himself into thinking it wasn't enough. There was never enough for him to feel as though he was fully prepared. This is one of the problems with the perfectionist mentality—the mind has a difficult time emphasizing what can be improved when it is so completely focused on everything that is not being done.

After a few weeks, I realized this assignment wasn't going to be completed. I adjusted and asked the player to imagine that he was no longer playing, but rather coaching in the NFL. I asked him to imagine that the one athlete he was responsible for had the exact same skill set as he did, and he needed to list for his athlete specifically what needed to be done each day to be fully prepared for game day. The kicker easily took to this assignment, and within a week he presented me with an itemized list of exactly what needed to be done for game-day success.

I asked him if he believed this plan would be enough for him. After a long pause, he let me know that he did believe it would be enough. Defining when "enough was enough" served him better than his previous quest for perfection. He immediately felt his stress and anxiety levels drop significantly. When he initially came to see me, he stated that his stress levels were "off the charts." Having a defined and doable daily plan put his stress levels at a much more manageable level. Interestingly, the list he created was actually less work than he was previously putting in, and over the few years we worked together, his kicking percentage even increased slightly.

PERFECTIONIST MENTALITY

1. Overlook successes
2. Focus on shortcomings

An individual with the perfectionist mentality is quick to dismiss what he or she has done well. He hits a home run, but then says, "Yeah, but my fielding was off today." She nails the presentation, but then says, "Yeah, but I wasn't totally prepared for that one question." He makes healthy food choices for the day, but then says, "Yeah, but I should have done a longer workout." When perfectionists do something well, they simply expect that of themselves and refuse to take any credit for a job well done.

When the NFL kicker nailed a long field goal, he didn't feel good about it for more than a moment because he felt like he *should* have made the field goal. It was merely expected. When something is done less than perfectly, a person with the perfectionist mentality focuses solely on the imperfection.

Are you the type of person who does 99 things well and one thing less than perfectly, only to beat yourself up for the one imperfection? If so, I want you to realize that doing so is a sure sign of mental weakness. It's good to have high expectations of yourself; however, focusing on the imperfections rather than on what you are doing well is a big mistake.

The perfectionist mentality is quite common, especially with talented individuals. Sports psychology and performance psychology textbooks all state that the perfectionist mentality is 100 percent counterproductive. That has not necessarily been my experience. I have seen individuals use the standard of perfection to promote growth at the lower levels of competition. As the level of competition increases, so too does the negative impact of the perfectionist mentality. Typically, the higher a person climbs on the ladder of success, the fewer the external pats on the back. At the higher levels of competition, a person is left with her own self-talk to determine self-confidence. If that self-talk has been shaped by a perfectionist mentality, anxiety and stress begin to increase, and performance and self-confidence begin to decrease.

As the level of competition increases, so too does the negative impact of the perfectionist mentality.

You might wonder how important self-confidence really is. Self-confidence is the number one variable for human performance. Remember, focusing on problems erodes self-confidence, while focusing on solutions grows it.

Self-Confidence and Performance

Let's say it again, *self-confidence is the number one variable for all human performance.* If an individual believes in her ability to accomplish something, then the likelihood of success increases significantly. If a person doesn't have self-confidence, producing desirable results proves to be much more difficult.

The perfectionist mentality destroys self-confidence at every level of performance, and the negative impact deepens as the level of competition increases. When your focus remains on where you fall short, you are constantly reminded of how *much* you fall short. When you are not in the habit of giving yourself credit for even the little things you've done well, you are not reminding yourself that you *can* be successful. Expectancy theory can work for or against your self-confidence. It is going to expand whatever you focus on, so it is crucial to make sure you are focusing on the right things.

The research on the importance of self-confidence first appeared in 1960 in the ground-breaking book *Psycho-Cybernetics* by Dr. Maxwell Maltz. Maltz said the following about self-confidence, or self-image as he called it:

1. A person will not outperform, nor will he underperform, his self-image for long.
2. A person develops self-image by how he consistently talks to himself about himself.
3. Most people have very low self-image because of the normal negative self-talk that goes on in one's head (perfectionism and problem-centric thought [PCT]).

Think of self-confidence as a thermostat. If you set the temperature at 72 degrees, the AC unit cools the house to 72 degrees. When the temp hits 71 degrees, the thermostat sends a message to the AC unit, saying we are good to go, and you can relax a bit. But once the house warms up to 73 degrees, the thermostat sends another message to the AC unit that the break is over, and you need to get back to work. This goes on all day long.

Your brain does the same thing. It wants your results to line up with wherever your self-confidence is set. If your belief in your ability to execute is high, you should achieve high results. If your self-image is set high, but you are not experiencing great results, you increase your motivation and effort to get the results. If your self-image is set low, and you are not experiencing great results, then things are in line. There is no motivation for change—you don't expect to get great results, so you don't. The world makes sense. Just like a thermostat, your effort and motivation either "kick on" or "kick off" when the temperature gets either higher or lower than the level where it is set. If your self-confidence is high, you are motivated to put in the effort to achieve your expected results. It's really that straightforward.

Perfectionists undermine themselves not because they have high expectations of themselves, but because they continually evaluate themselves in a very negative manner. They don't give themselves credit where credit is due, taking for granted the positive results and focusing only on the shortcomings. It takes great mental toughness to force yourself to actually recognize what you do well. Instead of focusing on the imperfections, the emphasis shifts to what you can do to improve. It's actually quite paradoxical. If you truly want to be perfect, then you must stop thinking like a perfectionist. Those who have learned to replace perfectionist thoughts with a focus on "What did I do well?" and "What do I want to improve?" have the greatest likelihood of finding those highest zones of performance.

So how do we make sure self-image is set high? According to Maltz, it's how we talk *to* ourselves *about* ourselves. You should be an expert by now on the effects of PCT. PCT does not set us up to focus on our successes. The natural course of thought for most people is negative and self-doubting.

Remember, mental toughness and an RSF mindset are abnormal and take work and practice. If we want to perform at a high level consistently, we need to have the self-confidence of someone who performs at a high level. To have the self-confidence of someone who performs at a high level, we need to be accountable for maintaining our self-confidence ourselves. You cannot afford to wait for someone to tell you that you have done something well. Instead, you must train yourself to recognize those done-wells yourself. Other people are going to become less and less likely to do it for you as the levels of performance and competition increase.

Focus on "What did I do well?" and
"What do I want to improve?"

Think about it this way: Your perfectionist mentality is like having a boss who looks the other way every time you do something well; however, each time you do something short of perfect, the boss is right there, giving you an earful about your mistake. It wouldn't take long before your self-confidence was shot. Now imagine you have a boss who gives you a genuine pat on the back for what you do well and also pushes you to make improvements where needed. For which boss would you rather work, and for which boss would you perform better?

These done-wells are not the equivalent of participation trophies, but rather honest, positive feedback for a good performance. Not everyone deserves a medal. If you haven't put in the effort, and if you don't deserve to win, then you shouldn't be rewarded. However, if you are doing something well, it is a really good idea to recognize those positives so as to reinforce that behavior. I am not talking about throwing yourself a parade or printing T-shirts in your honor, just the simple mental recognition, "Hey, I did this well today." Learning to recognize your done-wells daily is the first step for anyone wanting to develop mental toughness.

Learning to recognize your done-wells daily is the first
step for anyone wanting to develop mental toughness.

IMPROVEMENT IS THE KEY

I can't tell you how often I hear some version of "I'm not good at *x*," "I've never been a person who *y*," or "I always end up failing at *z*." Anytime someone gives me an excuse for not being perfect, I remind him or her that when a person learns to emphasize *improvement* over perfection, progress accelerates. Making the mental shift from focusing on what is not perfect about what you are doing to "What is one thing I am doing well?" or "What is one thing I can do to improve?" makes all the difference in the world. It is easy to think of traits or characteristics as fixed to avoid having to put in the work to change them. The next time you catch yourself thinking or saying something negative about yourself, make it a point to first recognize something you are doing well. This simple little change done consistently will serve as a stable footing for building mental toughness.

When a person learns to emphasize improvement
over perfection, progress accelerates.

After I gave a speech a few years ago, one of the attendees came up to me to discuss how he had implemented some of the fundamentals he had read in a few of my books. I was thrilled to hear he had made a few crucial changes in his life, and he was experiencing a great deal of career success. Without realizing the negative self-talk that was swirling through his mind from this next statement, he added, "I've never been a very good leader, but we've managed to be successful in spite of that." I stopped him and said, "I'm so happy to hear about all the great work you've been doing. Now, don't ever say that again." He chuckled, and I told him I was serious. I challenged him to replace the statement, "I've never been a very good leader" with "I'm working on becoming a great leader." The latter statement has truth, and it allows him to show up to the fight. Allowing yourself to focus on your imperfections keeps you on the problem side of the mental chalkboard. Don't let your mind become so focused on what isn't perfect that you lose the ability to realize and take action on what can be improved. It all begins by recognizing those perfectionist thoughts. Don't be the type of person who does 99 things well and one thing less than perfectly, and then overlooks all the positives only to focus on the imperfection. Remember, doing so is a sure sign of mental weakness. Stop beating yourself up, and stop trying to be perfect. Focus instead on improvement. There is always a way to improve. Always.

Stop beating yourself up, and stop trying to be perfect. Focus instead on improvement.

Remember Rachel from Chapter 7? She was always the A-student, always working for the gold star, and always going the extra mile. This sounds great on paper, and for most of her life, this had worked well for her. She was the quintessential "teacher's pet." Her superiors loved her drive and passion, and Rachel loved that they loved it. She was used to being adored. Rachel learned about herself early on that she was dependable, motivated, and smart. She was told this all the time.

Fast-forward 15 years, and by the time Rachel came to me, she was perpetually frazzled, discouraged, and depressed. What happened in between? She had grown up her whole life *knowing* that she had what it takes to do anything, and she got confirmation of that from her peers and superiors all the time. Rachel did not think she had to worry about self-confidence because everyone on the outside told her constantly how great she was. In fact, when her teachers would tell her how proud they were of her, she would usually respond with something like, "Thank you, but I really struggle with *x*." What's more, this type of response would usually garner her even more praise from her teachers. "That Rachel, she is so bright and so humble."

As Rachel's level of success increased, just like the NFL kicker, the negative impact of being a perfectionist began making deeper and deeper cuts. Even though both were experiencing external success, neither had learned how to give *themselves* credit for done-wells. They both had the perfectionist mentality and both ended up miserable.

When it comes to the perfectionist mentality, expectancy theory really puts the nail in the coffin. Focusing on shortcomings creates *more* shortcomings. How easy is it to excel when you are constantly focused on everything you are doing wrong? It's nearly impossible.

Trust me, I used to be a perfectionist as well. I have problems just like anyone else, but now I just don't become bogged down by them. When bad things happen in my life, I have trained myself to identify first what I am doing well, and then what I can do to make my situation better. I have learned to chip away at whatever adversity life throws my way by using the RSF tool (*What is one thing I can do that could make this better?*). Because I have been working on developing solution-focused brain circuitry, it has become so much easier to forgive myself for not being perfect, while improving my ability to become relentless toward improvement. If your mind is not trained to focus on what you are doing well, it will be focused on all those things you are not doing well, and that is not good.

RSF MINDSET

Emphasizing improvement over perfection is a defining characteristic of the RSF mindset. At every level of competition, the RSF mindset outperforms the perfectionist mentality. There are two characteristics associated with the RSF mindset:

1. Learn to recognize done-wells
2. Have an obsession for *improvement*

Recognize Done-Wells

Although it seems simple and maybe even a bit soft to think about what you are doing well, it is actually quite difficult and requires major mental toughness. Over the years, Ellen and I have worked with some extremely tough individuals—mixed martial arts fighters, NFL standouts, Olympians, Navy SEALs, and CEOs—and for all, the first fundamental of developing mental toughness is learning to recognize done-wells.

Instead of being quick to blow off successes, an individual who has developed the RSF mindset *forces* herself to recognize them. This is neither normal nor natural. Let's take this opportunity to define what qualifies as an actual done-well—anything that promotes personal or professional health counts. No matter how many days in a row you have done it or how small the impact, if it improves personal or professional health even slightly, it is a done-well.

Here are a few examples of done-wells:

- Arrived at my desk three minutes early
- Had great energy on my calls today
- Made one prospect contact today
- Had two cups of coffee instead of three
- Worked out
- Texted my wife, "I love you"
- Spent five minutes connecting with my daughter after school
- Had an AFD (alcohol-free day)

- Did my shoulder stretches
- Skipped dessert

You might look at these done-wells and think, "What type of person needs to recognize such small and unimportant accomplishments?" Well, that person is me. Those are my last few days of done-wells. No matter how small the impact or how many days you have already done it, if it is good for you, it is a done-well.

It's not the size of the done-well that matters, but the fact that you are forcing your mind to think about what you are doing well, as opposed to the normal PCT or perfectionist type of thinking. Recognizing done-wells on a consistent basis creates new neural patterns. You are teaching yourself a new and improved way of thinking. The more you think about done-wells, the more natural this becomes, and the more your self-confidence grows. That which you focus on expands.

---

*It's not the size of the done-well that matters,
but the fact that you are forcing your mind
to think about what you are doing well.*

Practice recognizing a few done-wells right now. Think for a moment about three things you have done well in the past 24 hours. Use the following space to write them down:

- _____
- _____

- _____

If you thought to yourself, "I didn't do anything major today," realize that is your perfectionist mentality. Don't let yourself think that if you didn't do something perfectly or something major like curing cancer that it shouldn't count. Thinking in that way is a sign of mental weakness. Recognizing your done-wells requires mental toughness. If you haven't already written three down, please do so now.

Have an Obsession for Improvement

The second characteristic of the RSF mindset is having an obsession for improvement. Keep in mind, *improvement* is another word for *solution*. All improvements are solutions. Instead of trying to be perfect, an individual with an RSF mindset relentlessly pursues *improvement*. When a person thinks about solutions, it typically means there must be a problem. But having the RSF mindset isn't about only getting better when there are problems, but also getting better in good times.

All improvements are solutions.

On March 19, 2006, I had been asked by the St. Louis Cardinals to fly out to Jupiter, Florida, for what in reality was an interview for the Director of Sport Psychology position. I was given 10 minutes to convince manager Tony LaRussa and the team that I would be able to help them develop the mental toughness they needed to win a World Series—something they hadn't done in 24 years. At that point in my career, I hadn't written any books or worked with any professional sports teams. I was essentially a nobody, and I found myself in the clubhouse presenting to All-Star and future Hall of Fame players such as Jim Edmonds, Scott Rolen, David Eckstein, Chris Carpenter, Adam Wainwright, Albert Pujols, and Yadier Molina. I was presenting research on something I had created a few years earlier called the Mental Workout. After about five or six minutes into my presentation, I saw something that totally shocked me. All these superstar players and coaches started taking notes.

I was in total awe of the fact that they were already some of the best players and coaches in the world, and they were still searching for a way to get better. From that moment on, I began noticing the same pattern with those who were most successful. I first heard the phrase "obsession for improvement" several years later while working with one of the best professional hockey players in the world. I asked him why he felt he had been able to become as great as he was for as long as he had, and I will never forget his response. He said, "I have an obsession for improvement." When he said it, I immediately knew that had been exactly what I had seen during my time with the St. Louis Cardinals and with many of the other extremely successful clients with whom I had worked. The most successful people in life have an obsession for improvement. They are constantly focused on solutions.

In the past few years, I have seen more and more people talking about this "obsession for improvement" concept; unfortunately, most are doing it wrong. Most apply the concept by taking the perfectionist approach of trying to improve everything, all the way, all the time. As we have discussed, doing it that way is the perfect recipe for inconsistency and disaster. Those who enjoy the most success realize that the obsession for improvement is about having just *one* thing at which you are trying to get just a little bit better. Not 10 things or even 2 things, but just 1 thing you are trying to improve.

The most successful people in life have an obsession for improvement.

Here are some examples of what my one thing to improve has been over the past six days:

- Fill last two seats for upcoming coaching event
- Catch up on emails, texts, and voicemails before leaving town
- Be more connected with my wife

- Complete both sets of shoulder exercises
- Have an AFD (alcohol-free day)
- Reduce carbs (half of normal portion)

Take a minute to think about the one thing right now that you want to improve. To make it easier, use the time frame of the next 24 hours. Write it down in the following space.

One thing I want to improve in the next 24 hours:

_____

Focusing on what you want to improve instead of what you screwed up is a very subtle, but *very* important distinction. Most people get so consumed with what they aren't doing well that they put little or no energy into what they can do to improve. If you are thinking about the mistake you made, you cannot be focused on what or how you can get better. Expectancy theory and PCT ensure that if you spend too much time on your screw-ups, then you will end up in a PCT tornado, and as we have discussed, that can be very difficult to escape.

I have spoken about developing the RSF mentality at many corporate events, and it is not uncommon for me to get a comment or question from the crowd about the importance of "spending time to really understand your problems so you can figure out how to get past them." I actually appreciate getting this comment because I know this is something a lot of people may be wondering about. This seems logical, doesn't it? When you screw up, you should analyze *why* and *how* you screwed up, so that you don't do it again. The reality is, our brains don't work like this. It may seem like you can objectively dive into your screw-ups and problems to better understand them and move forward, but the more you dive in, the harder it is to get out. This doesn't mean you put on rose-colored glasses and turn a blind eye to your problems or mistakes, but it does require you to *immediately* move to

"What can I do to improve next time?" Does this mean that you may not come up with as good a solution than if you had really analyzed your mistake? Maybe. But that is so much less important than not getting sucked into the problem focus.

To the engineers and accountants who are reading this and thinking, "This guy clearly doesn't know what he is talking about. I need to fully examine the problem before I can even begin thinking about a solution," all I ask is that you experiment with this. Next time you find yourself experiencing a negative emotion, recognize that is your PCT alarm. Instead of putting energy into "fully understanding" the problem, immediately attack the problem by making yourself answer the RSF tool question within 60 seconds—*"What is one thing I can do that could make this better?"* If you must analyze the problem, make it a point to do so for only 60 seconds at the most. Please give this a fair shot. Don't half-heartedly run this experiment; be *relentless.* I am a gambling man, and I will bet on you every time with this approach. Trust me, you will see the benefits of focusing on improvements instead of understanding problems.

Remember that if your first solution or idea for improvement doesn't get you all the way there, then you just come up with a second and a third and a fourth and so on. Keep yourself on the solution side of the mental chalkboard. If you get sucked into the problem side of the board and don't even get to the first solution, then you have lost before you have even started. It is *very* easy to get sucked into your problem. By the time you get out of it, you are miles behind and will have likely done a lot of damage to your self-confidence in the process. This is why not allowing yourself more than 60 seconds on the problem side of the mental chalkboard is so crucial.

FROM PERFECTION TO PERFORMANCE

When the NFL kicker first began writing on paper three things he had done well, he called me and asked, "Am I supposed to feel better every time I write those done-wells down?" It was the right question to ask, and I immediately realized that I hadn't truly managed his expectations. I responded, "Writing the done-wells on paper probably won't make you immediately feel anything. Doing so is all about retraining your brain to think more effectively when things aren't going well. If you commit to recognizing those done-wells now, I can promise you will feel much better on the tough days, and little by little you should notice less stress and anxiety."

Think of it like a piggy bank. You don't necessarily feel better each time you make a deposit of a few pennies; however, over time, the money adds up. When you do need to dip into it, you are certainly glad you had been putting money in consistently. Much like that piggy bank, the more consistently you recognize your done wells, the better you feel about yourself. One of my players from the St. Louis Cardinal days said it to me this way: "I sure am glad you stayed on me about writing down what I did well on a daily basis because on those days I go 0 for 4, those days are the days I really need it. It just totally stops me from doing what I used to do, which is beat the hell out of myself and end up going into a nosedive."

For the NFL kicker, instead of dreading practice and game day, he once again began experiencing joy for playing the game he had grown up loving. Spending so much time chasing perfection and focusing on what he wasn't doing well sucked the enjoyment out of playing and competing. Recognizing done-wells slowly but surely helped him feel like he was becoming himself again and getting his life back.

Every time you force yourself to write down things you have done well and what you want to improve, you are literally training your mind to focus on solutions rather than problems. New neural pathways are forming, and this will serve as rocket fuel for cultivating self-confidence and growth.

RSF AND INTEGRITY

You developed your framework in Chapter 7, which culminated in your two process goals (personal and professional). The next step is to *execute.* This may seem obvious, but this is worth mentioning because it is incredibly common for people to develop a game plan, but never execute it. If you are one of those people, then realize that it is more than likely your perfectionist tendencies are what caused you to fall short. Recognizing done-wells and focusing on improvements rather than failures is the cornerstone of developing the mental toughness needed to actually execute and follow through on your daily commitments. Remember, knowing something does nothing. *Knowing* you should stop focusing on problems and beating yourself up is meaningless if you don't *do* something about it.

We want you to start applying the RSF mindset to your one personal and one professional process goal that you developed in Chapter 7. Remember that these two process goals represent the integrity piece of your framework (i.e., doing what you need to do on a daily basis that will get you where you want to go). We want you to form the habit of recognizing what you did well toward completing and executing on your process goals, and if you didn't nail those process goals, instead of beating yourself up, simply identify one thing you can adjust that will increase the likelihood of nailing it tomorrow. Use the RSF tool (*What is one thing I can do that could make this better?*) to help find this adjustment or improvement.

The goal for completing your two most important process goals should be 90 percent completion or better. You do not need to be perfect in completing those daily process goals. Working with highly successful people for the past 25 years has taught me that if you nail your most important activities 90 percent of the time or better, you will really like the results. It is important to remember the quote by one of the greatest athletes of all time, the great golfer Ben Hogan: "I stopped trying to do a great many difficult things perfectly because it had become clear in my mind that this ambitious over-thoroughness was neither possible nor advisable, or even necessary."

Again, do not worry about adopting the RSF mentality for your entire life. Focus on applying RSF only to your two process goals. When you experience success in these two areas, RSF carries over into other areas. Keep it simple. Recognize the little things you are doing to help with the execution of your two process goals, and continue to ask yourself how you can get just a little bit better at them.

RSF MAY EVEN SAVE YOUR LIFE

"Dad, you need to stop moving. Don't move."

Those were the words Tony Christensen heard his 16-year-old son Aiden say to him on March 28, 2018. Thirty minutes earlier, Tony, his wife, Allison, Aiden, and one of Aiden's friends had climbed into their 2018 Yukon Denali at their Humboldt, Iowa, home for the drive to Breckenridge, Colorado. The family was excited to be going on a ski vacation for spring break. Unfortunately, they would not make it to Colorado. They wouldn't even make it out of Iowa.

Twenty-five miles into the trip, a drunk driver with three times the legal intoxication limit hit the Christensens' car head-on while traveling at 60-plus miles per hour. Tony swerved at the last second in an attempt to avoid the crash, saving his family from major injury, but absorbing the direct impact on his side of the vehicle. Allison, Aiden, and his friend all walked away from the crash with minor injuries.

Tony and the other driver weren't so lucky. The driver of the other car was instantly killed, and Tony's injuries were severe. His spine was fractured in three places (C2, C3, and L5), and he had an open pelvic fracture, which is usually fatal. He had broken his left hip, sternum, leg, foot, toes, and eight ribs. His MCL, ACL, PCL, and meniscus were all torn, and he had a compound fracture on his humerus. However, most concerning of all was a large piece of metal from his engine block had impaled his left calf and severed a major artery. It was preventing Tony from moving.

I first met Tony Christensen in 2016 when he attended a two-day workshop I was cohosting with my friend and business partner Tom Bartow. I was immediately impressed with Tony's work ethic and positive energy. He was a very quick study with RSF and the idea of mental training. At that point in time, Tony had set a goal to become one of the top producers in his firm. With his knowledge and approach of "always taking care of the client," I felt very confident that he had an excellent chance of hitting his goal. Little did either of us know that on the day of his accident, he would be just a couple hundred dollars short of achieving that very goal.

When Tony heard Aiden's words, "Dad, you need to stop moving. Don't move," he immediately knew there was a major problem. Tony immediately went into RSF mode, asking himself, *"What is one thing I can do right now to make this situation better?"* His first focus was on his breathing. He knew he was in trouble, and he had to stay calm and keep his focus on merely improving his current situation if he was going to live through this. Tony had been consistently doing the mental training in the form of the Mental Workout that you will learn in the final chapter to make RSF the norm for him, even in the face of such adversity.

Tony said:

> I knew I needed to get myself under control. I inhaled for seven seconds, held for three, then out for eight. I know you taught me to do the breath for 6-2-7, but what can I say—if that is good, then 7-3-8 must be better. One point that sticks in my mind about the accident is that I didn't stress. When I took the centering breath, the results were immediate. The biological changes enabled me to work on the cold and the pain. I am so glad I practiced that breath twice a day in my Mental Workout since sitting in the airport after attending your workshop.

After Tony got his breathing under control, he continued his focus on improving his current situation with his Mental Workout. Keep in mind, he knew if he allowed himself to focus on the entirety of his situation rather than the next solution, he would panic and go into shock. He recited his identity statement—"I share the love of my wife and my boys. I prepare and outwork other financial advisors to be a two-million-dollar producer. I eat right and work out hard enough to weigh 195 pounds." He then visualized the life he wanted to have in five years, his level of success, his health, and most important, the relationships he wanted to have with his wife and children. Then he began visualizing himself dealing with the pain that he was in, reminding himself that the pain was temporary and that he wouldn't allow it to kill him. He repeated his identity statement one more time and then concentrated on his breathing.

Tony waited for an entire hour before the Jaws of Life released him from his mangled vehicle. He had a keen awareness that controlling his thoughts was the key to his survival. He controlled his mind, and his body listened. He focused on breathing and sitting motionless, battling the cold and the pain by forcing his mind to positive visions of the way he wanted his life to turn out, and how he would survive this accident and become even stronger than before. To the amazement of every doctor and paramedic, Tony stayed alive through the night. And then he made it through the next day, and the day after that.

Surviving the actual accident was just the beginning for Tony. In the 18 months after the accident, he has had eight surgeries and has spent close to a thousand hours in physical therapy. It has been a long, hard road. All of Tony's doctors and physical therapists agree that he should not have survived the accident, and even if he had, he most certainly should have been paralyzed. No one truly knows how powerful the mind is, and Tony will be the first to tell you that in his case, RSF saved his life.

Today, Tony still goes to physical therapy, and it is highly likely that there are more surgeries to come, but he keeps his focus on his next inch of improvement. Because of his RSF mindset, he is alive, and he improves a little bit every day. He told me that he was once again approaching the goal of becoming one of the top producers in his firm, and that if I wrote in the book that "He was on track to reach it," he would be sure to do so by the time the book is published.

Tony Christensen is relentless, and it literally saved his life. My bet is that by the time you read this story, he has already achieved his goal. In the next chapter, you will learn the two most effective tools to internalize the RSF mindset. Retraining your mind through these two tools will cause RSF to become your norm. While RSF is not always a matter of life or death, its effect on your quality of life can be just as impactful.

Ellen and I want this chapter to boil down to one thing: Each day we want you to be clear about what your two most important activities are and then execute daily through the lens of "What did I do well in terms of getting those two activities done?" and "What is one thing I can improve to be even just a touch better at those two activities tomorrow?" This may sound simple, but it will not be easy. The final chapter will provide you with the concrete tools (the Mental Workout and Success Log) to help train your mind to commit to RSF consistently.

③ THINGS TO *KNOW*

1. A perfectionist mentality causes you to overlook success and focus on imperfections, while an RSF mindset enables you to recognize done-wells and develop an obsession for improvement.
2. Focusing on problems erodes self-confidence, while thinking about solutions grows self-confidence. All improvements are solutions.
3. Self-confidence is the number one variable for performance. A person neither outperforms nor underperforms his self-confidence for long.

① THING TO *DO*

Schedule It or Forget It

Take a few minutes now to determine when you will complete your two process goals. If your personal process goal is to exercise for 30 minutes five days per week, block off the days and times on your calendar. If your professional process goal is to reach out to five new prospects daily, block out the time in your calendar to devote to this. Be sure to choose the time when it is easiest for you to get these done.

Next, set a reminder on your phone to alert you each day when it's time to attack your two process goals. Then make the commitment to complete those tasks early or on time. When your phone reminds you that it's time, I can pretty much guarantee you will be in the middle of other things, or you may just not feel like doing it. If you say to yourself, "I will do it later," you are making a huge mistake. "I'll do it later" is psychological code for "it's not that important," and if you tell yourself something isn't important, it is only a matter of time before doing it becomes inconsistent. When it's time to complete process goals, tell yourself this is the absolute most important thing you can be doing in life, and then . . . *do it* immediately. Doing so will help you realize: *you are unstoppable.*

9

The Mental Workout and Success Log

Train Yourself to Become Unstoppable

Kelly Hall-Tompkins is recognized as one of the top violinists in the world. She is known for *becoming* the music on stage, from the beautifully sublime to the dramatically intense. Each time Kelly performs at Carnegie Hall or any great concert hall in the world, her violin is a seamless extension of herself. With each stroke of the bow, she draws forth beauty, power, and virtuosity. Kelly attacks the music with "searing intensity" (*American Record Guide*). She is acclaimed by the *New York Times* as "the versatile violinist who makes the music come alive." For 13 months on Broadway, Kelly was the Fiddler in *Fiddler on the Roof*. She has been the featured subject on NBC's *Today Show* with Harry Smith. She has performed all over the world and has exceeded one million YouTube views. In 2018, she was chosen by the *New York Times* as the "New Yorker of the Year." In addition, Kelly is a dedicated humanitarian. She founded and directs Music Kitchen—Food for the Soul, which has brought almost 100 chamber music performances to New York City and Los Angeles homeless shelters to date, and has been featured in the *New York Times*, on CBSNews.com, and on ABCNews.com. And, by the way, Kelly studies and speaks eight languages.

Saying Kelly Hall-Tomkins is a success is an understatement. But she is human. I say this with all seriousness. Most of us look at individuals like Kelly and think they are robots or aliens from another world. I have had the great pleasure of knowing Kelly for eight years, and I assure you she works for everything she has achieved. She is the epitome of *relentless*. I have worked with many top performers, and Kelly stands out as one of the most focused and hardworking individuals I know. What most people don't see about Kelly is the level of preparation she puts into each and every day.

Kelly spends five hours daily in physical preparation. Typically, she spends an hour or so working out and another four hours in rehearsal or practice. In addition, she invests roughly 15 minutes daily on mental preparation. (Kelly devotes a bit more time on mental prep to better deal with the intense pressure of her high-level performances.)

I certainly wouldn't expect most people to spend the same kind of time Kelly puts into her preparation. Keep in mind, her art requires tremendous precision, and she is one of the best in the world. Kelly completes daily the two extremely important tasks for training the RSF mindset: the Mental Workout and the Success Log. These are the most scientifically proven exercises to help you develop RSF and mental toughness. The good news is that mentally training yourself for increased success, happiness, and health using these two tools only requires less than three minutes per day.

PREPARATION: THE MENTAL WORKOUT

The first method of training for the RSF mindset is the Mental Workout, which prepares you to win your fight against problem-centric thought (PCT) every day. I first developed the Mental Workout in 1999, just as I was finishing graduate school. I used it with professional athletes, and it is what propelled me to being recognized as one of the top sport psychology consultants in the world in a very short period of time. The Mental Workout was the first mental training tool of its kind that taught athletes exactly what to do to develop mental toughness in high-level competition.

I developed the Mental Workout while sitting on my deck, preparing for graduate school comps—the comprehensive exam I needed to pass to earn my doctorate. Comps are a 40-hour week of testing, during which anything learned over the previous four years of schooling is fair game. It is a grueling process, to say the least. While I was studying during the last few days before comps week, the only room in my home that was big enough to lay out all the textbooks, practical guides, and notes I had used in my graduate studies was the deck at the back of my house. As I sat in the afternoon sun, going from one resource to the next, trying to commit the information to memory, I had a frightening thought: "I have all this education and knowledge. What in the heck am I going to do with it to actually get a return on this investment of time and money?" Keep in mind, I was 29 years old and about to no longer be a student for the first time since beginning first grade. It suddenly hit me that making money had not been covered in any of my classes, and I had taken them all at this point.

Little did I know that the next 45 minutes would possibly be the most important of my career. I first realized that the job of a sport psychologist was very similar to that of a physical therapist or trainer. If a person wants to strengthen his body, he goes to see a trainer and is taught the most scientifically proven methods of building muscle efficiently. I knew the brain was like a muscle. It needs to be exercised to remain healthy and to perform optimally. Why shouldn't I approach mental training the same way? At that very moment in time, I was surrounded by all the most up-to-date scientific and practical information available on how to most effectively train the mind for increased performance. That was the genesis of the Mental Workout.

The Mental Workout is a five-step process that takes one minute and 40 seconds to complete. Doing the Mental Workout daily not only helps increase mental toughness, focus, and confidence, it also significantly speeds up the process of developing the RSF mindset. Mental Workouts are the equivalent of hitting the weight room for your mind. They are the most effective method of ensuring you are mentally ready to attack and win on a daily basis. You must train your mind to leverage the good in your life. Otherwise, PCT will ruin your perspective by tainting everything with a negative filter.

THE MENTAL WORKOUT

1. **Centering breath:** Breathe in for six seconds, hold for two seconds, and then exhale for seven seconds.
2. **Identity statement:** Say to yourself your personal mantra of who you want to be and how you want your life to go. For example, my identity statement is, "I outwork the competition every day. I am the most effective performance coach and speaker in the country, and I experience true love as a husband and father."
3. **Personal highlight reel:**
   Vision (30 seconds): Spend 30 seconds visualizing your vision of self-image from Chapter 7. Remember, your vision of self-image is a detailed image of who you want to be and what you want your life to be like in 3 to 10 years. Spend 30 seconds visualizing yourself as this person and living that desired life.

Integrity (30 seconds): Visualize for another 30 seconds what you need to do in the upcoming day to best position yourself to make your vision of self-image your actual reality. Be sure always to include seeing yourself complete your two most important activities daily (your process goals from Chapter 7).

4. **Identity statement:** Repeat your identity statement to yourself.

5. **Centering breath:** Once again, breathe in for six seconds, hold for two seconds, and then exhale for seven seconds.

The Centering Breath

Pressure is everywhere. Whether you are preparing to make a big sale, interview for a job, or have a difficult conversation with your spouse or children, you feel the pressure associated with performance. From a scientific standpoint, the first physical response to pressure is the acceleration of your heart rate. Unfortunately, the elevated heart rate also sends a message to your brain that it should consider moving into "fight or flight." In this state, your brain loses its ability to have detailed thoughts. This is why people tend to talk faster and often say goofy things when they are nervous. Rushing almost always has a negative impact on performance. The more elevated the heart rate, the less likely the brain remains at an optimal level of functioning. Trying to perform at a high level with your heart racing is like trying to perform intricate surgery in an ambulance barreling down a bumpy road. It's usually, if not always, a losing and frustrating proposition.

An effective way to control your heart rate is by using the centering breath. The centering breath is a purposeful, deep breath that lets you keep your heart rate under control so you can slow down and perform at a more effective pace. Centering breaths physiologically decrease your heart rate and help you better deal with pressure by staying in control of your thoughts.

Take a moment now to practice a centering breath:

1. Breathe in for six seconds.
2. Hold for two seconds.
3. Exhale for seven seconds.

As you take this centering breath, you will feel control set in. It feels good, doesn't it? When you use a centering breath at the start and end of your Mental Workout, you bring your heart rate under control, better allowing you to maintain thought control. In that place, your mind can settle into its most optimal performance level as you visualize and mentally rehearse what you are trying to accomplish, and what it takes to get there.

Identity Statement

The identity statement is a personal mantra designed to improve how you see yourself. It should be tailored to the person you hope to become. It is important to develop a self-image that is aligned with what you want to accomplish in life. When you consistently say your identity statement to yourself, you begin to believe it. Consistently suggesting to yourself that you have the RSF mindset and that you always focus on solutions increases the likelihood of high accomplishment. Through repitition of your identity statement, you begin to create your desired image.

Consistently suggesting to yourself that you have the RSF mindset and that you always focus on solutions increases the likelihood of high accomplishment.

Here are some examples of identity statements from some of my clients:

- I have the RSF mindset, and I always focus on solutions. I am a million-dollar producer.
- I am ferocious. I am a solution-focused machine. My happiness, health, and success are in abundance.
- I am full of positive energy, and I focus only on solutions. Every day I am happy, healthy, and successful.
- I am healthy, confident, and strong. I attack every day. I am unstoppable.

Your identity statement is your mantra that confirms you *are* a person who is successful and gets things done. Repeating your identity statement twice in each of your Mental Workouts locks in your propensity to become your potential. It builds your confidence and focuses your mind on achievement, rather than on failure or excuses. To create your identity statement, follow three simple guidelines:

Guideline 1: Think about the one thing personally and the one thing professionally you most want to be or have. For example, "I am the most effective performance coach and speaker in the country," "I am a solution-focused machine," or "I experience true health and happiness with my family."

Guideline 2: Identity statements are best if stated in three sentences or less. Force yourself to keep it short, sweet, and to the point.

Guideline 3: Use "I am" language, indicating to yourself that you have already accomplished or become your statement. It's much better to say, "I am ..." instead of "I am going to become ..." or

"I will be. . . ." Doing so speeds up the process of you owning and living up to it.

Take a moment right now and create your identity statement.

_____

_____

Personal Highlight Reel

Your personal highlight reel consists of approximately 60 seconds of visualization that we will break down into two separate parts. In part one, spend the first 30 seconds watching a mental video of your vision of self-image from Chapter 7, a detailed visualization of who you want to be and how you want your life to look 3 to 10 years in the future. In the second part of your personal highlight reel, dedicate the next 30 seconds to mentally seeing yourself attack and win the upcoming 24 hours. Be sure to reserve time to successfully complete your two most important tasks (process goals from Chapter 7), seeing them happen at the time you have planned to get them done. Pay attention to feeling good about getting them done and completing them with great energy, and then soaring into the rest of your day with confidence and momentum. Doing so greatly increases the likelihood of creating consistency around getting the most important things done daily. Over time this will significantly increase confidence and results, reinforcing the importance of and your ability to develop the RSF mindset.

Jack Nicklaus, quite possibly the greatest golfer of all time, explains his visualization work in the following way:

> I never hit a shot, not even in practice, without having a very sharp, in-focus picture of it in my head. It's like a color movie. First, I see the ball where I want it to finish, nice and white and sitting up high on bright green grass. Then the scene

quickly changes, and I see the ball going there: its path, trajectory, and shape, and even its behavior on landing.

The research on visualization suggests that a person cannot be performing at his or her potential without visualizing on a consistent basis. You must visualize regularly if you want to excel. Visualization trains your mind to stay focused on your control points. Here are a few simple guidelines that maximize its effectiveness.

You must visualize regularly if you want to excel.

Guideline 1: First person. Visualizing from the first-person vantage point means looking at the video through your own eyes, so you see the things you would actually see while performing the task or skill. If your professional process goal is to meet face-to-face with five clients per week, and you know you have one of those sales meeting in the upcoming day, visualize exactly what you would see, say, and feel while sitting in your seat, looking across the table at your client. Visualizing from the first-person perspective helps make the mental image a three-dimensional experience that feels real. This increases your confidence and skill most efficiently.

Guideline 2: Feel it. The video you play in your head needs to capture the emotional experience you want to have. Remember, self-confidence is the number one variable for performance, so be certain to imagine feeling confident in your visualization. Doing so significantly increases the likelihood of actually being confident come "go time."

Guideline 3: Desired speed. Make sure to watch your mental clip at the speed you want your performance to be. If you rush through visualization, you will likely rush your performance.

Likewise, if you visualize in slow motion, you may teach yourself to perform slowly.

Guideline 4: Short bursts. You may be wondering how you can visualize a 30-minute presentation, a 5-minute sales call, or a 2-minute script at real speed if you have only a 30-second block within your Mental Workout. That's a good question. You'll need to pick the most important moments within those events (5 to 10 seconds each) to run through in your visualization clips. Many people visualize in generalities, not realizing that this is far less effective than visualizing the details. The key is to visualize *specific* moments of success that will most cause your overall success. Remember, this is a "highlight reel." Just as a baseball player doesn't need to visualize an entire game's worth of performance, pick only the most important moments of your performance to visualize.

Spending 60 seconds visualizing (30 seconds of vision and 30 seconds of integrity) in the first person, feeling confident, running the reels at the desired speed, and seeing the highlights of performance in short bursts significantly increase your chances for success.

Once you have run through your personal highlight reel in your mind, simply repeat your identity statement to yourself, and then finish your Mental Workout with a final centering breath.

OK, now let's practice. And yes, I am aware you don't feel prepared to go through this. I get it, but I also know that if you don't do it right now, you may likely never do it. So let's run through one right now. I will help guide you.

The first thing I want you to do is to take a centering breath. Breathe in for six seconds. Hold for two seconds. Breathe out for seven seconds.

Now repeat in your head an identity statement. If you haven't already created one for yourself, choose from one of the following four. Once you have picked the one you like, simply say it to yourself in your head. You don't need to say it out loud.

- I have the RSF mindset, and I always focus on solutions. I am a million-dollar producer.
- I am ferocious. I am a solution-focused machine. My happiness, health, and success are in abundance.
- I am full of positive energy, and I focus only on solutions. Every day I am happy, healthy, and successful.
- I am healthy, confident, and strong. I attack every day. I am unstoppable.

You are already 40 percent of the way finished. Next, I want you to spend 30 seconds thinking about where you want your life to be in 3 to 10 years (your vision of self-image). Remember, you have already thought through this in Chapter 7 and written down a start on pages 158–159. The main goal here is to be specific. Using your vision of self-image from Chapter 7 as a reference, identify at least one thing you want to have in your life in the future. For example, you may see yourself pulling into the driveway of your beautiful house before the sun goes down, signifying that you have experienced career success and great work-life balance; or you may see yourself laughing with your spouse at a nice dinner that indicates you have built a fulfilling and loving relationship; or you may see yourself waking up early and enjoying your morning workout and being happy with what you see in the mirror, symbolizing that you have consistently prioritized your health over the years. Each day you do this, you begin to fill in more and more pieces of the puzzle from your vision of self-image, and you may even add to it. You eventually get the entire 30 seconds clearly and specifically focused on the life you want. Again, for now, let's just get a start.

If you didn't do the work to complete yours in Chapter 7, just spend 30 seconds thinking about what you want your life to be in 3 to 10 years. Don't be tempted to spend more than 30 seconds to get it perfect right now. Perfection is neither possible nor necessary. Anything you just visualized is a win. When you invest a little time each day working on this, you eventually get better and better at it. Visualizing specifically what you want from life makes your future even brighter.

Next, let's invest another 30 seconds visualizing the upcoming 24 hours. Remind yourself of what your two process goals are, and then see yourself completing them at the time you have committed to getting them done. Again, let's underscore the importance of just getting started here. Don't let concerns of doing it perfectly stop you from doing it at all. Merely let your mind think through your upcoming day, and visualize those two most important activities that better position you to get where you hope to be in the future. For example, you may see yourself waking up before the alarm and having a good workout, or getting your most important sales calls done soon after you arrive at the office, or putting 100 percent energy into preparing for a big presentation. Take 30 seconds now to visualize completing your two process goals, seeing them happen at the time you plan to get them done. Completing process goals "on time" helps reinforce psychologically that it is important.

You are almost finished. Now, repeat your identity statement to yourself. Next, to finish your first Mental Workout, simply take one more centering breath—breathe in for six seconds, hold for two seconds, and breath out for seven seconds.

Nice work. If you put any effort whatsoever into this, you made progress. Now, let's be clear. To develop the RSF mindset, you need to train your mind. I know you may not want to hear this, but I want you to go through your Mental Workout one more time. Doing so gives you a little jump start at this.

Please, for your own good, let's run through the Mental Workout one more time. Remember, you are worth it. By committing to the training, you will experience a significant increase in your personal health, happiness, and success. Take another one minute and 40 seconds right now to complete another Mental Workout.

1. **Centering breath:** Breathe in for six seconds, hold for two seconds, and then exhale for seven seconds.
2. **Identity statement:** Say to yourself your personal mantra of who you want to be and how you want your life to go.
3. **Vision and integrity highlight reel:**
   Vision (30 seconds): Spend 30 seconds visualizing your vision of self-image from Chapter 7 (a detailed image of who you want to be and what you want your life to be like in 3 to 10 years).
   Integrity (30 seconds): Visualize for another 30 seconds the two most important things (process goals) you need to do in the upcoming day to better move toward your vision of self-image.
4. **Identity statement:** Repeat your identity statement to yourself.
5. **Centering breath:** Once again, breathe in for six seconds, hold for two seconds, and then exhale for seven seconds.

Precisely when you complete the Mental Workout during your day is up to you. Many prefer to pin it to activities they do every day. For example, right after waking up in the morning, before exiting your car once you arrive at the office, or just before going to bed at night. Research suggests that visualization just before sleep integrates the visions into dreams and, therefore, raises the effectiveness of the visualization.

Others have found that the best results are achieved when the workout is completed within a few minutes of waking up, when the mind is clear and uncluttered. Most of our clients prefer to complete the Mental Workout within the first 30 minutes of waking up each morning, before the day really gets rolling, so they are fully ready for what lies ahead.

One hundred seconds, the time it takes to complete a Mental Workout, is about the time it takes to dry off after a shower or delete the junk mail from your inbox. Failure to complete the Mental Workout isn't necessarily a matter of lack of time as much as it is a lack of habit. Even though you may rationally agree that it's a great way to use one minute and 40 seconds of your time, you may forget to do it on a regular basis.

At the end of this chapter, we will ask you to reserve time within your daily calendar to complete your Mental Workout and lock it in as a new habit. By making the Mental Workout a habit, you set yourself on a winning trajectory toward developing mental toughness and focus as you have never experienced. By spending no more than 100 seconds per day on these workouts, you will experience *dramatic* and *immediate* improvements in your ability to achieve personal and professional success.

The Mental Workout is a critical component of preparing to be successful each day and developing an RSF mindset. The greatest pep talk in the world will not overcome biology. You need to complete Mental Workouts as part of your RSF training a minimum of three days a week to experience the positive new rewiring of your mind.

EVALUATION: SUCCESS LOG

Kelly Hall-Tompkins prepared for her rehearsals and performances each day with a Mental Workout, but just as critical to her mental game was the way she trained herself to evaluate her performance. Before working with me, like most high-level performers, Kelly had learned to evaluate herself using the perfectionist mentality—honing in on her shortcomings and being quick to dismiss her successes. Kelly would fixate on what went wrong in a performance. Even though no one in the audience would have likely picked up on her performance as anything less than extraordinary, she would become consumed with anything less than perfect. During one of our first meetings, I asked Kelly, "After listening to your students play, would you comment only on what went wrong with their performance?" Her response surprised us both: "I would never teach with that perspective. In a master class as a featured guest artist, I always recognize a student's strengths *before* zeroing in on their challenges, and I don't know why I didn't catch it for myself."

Once Kelly began the daily practice of evaluating herself through the RSF lens, she began to see significant improvements. "A big component of dramatically improving my ability to perform under pressure, my business successes, and most important, my joy in life is making sure to count done-wells in a daily capacity."

The daily practice that Kelly is referring to comes in the form of what I call Success Logs. In the previous chapter, we covered the importance of recognizing done-wells and focusing on improvement over perfection—the two components of the RSF mentality—but without a concrete tool to do so, you will likely fall back into the perfectionist mentality. Success Logs are the second tool critical for developing and maintaining RSF.

Let's dive into what is involved in completing a Success Log.

SUCCESS LOG

1. What three things did I do well in the previous 24 hours?
2. On a 10-point scale, how well did I do completing my professional process goal?
3. On a 10-point scale, how well did I do completing my personal process goal?
4. What is one thing I want to improve in the upcoming 24 hours?
5. What is one action step I can take to help make the improvement?
6. On a 10-point scale, how well did I do with RSF today?

These six simple questions, which should not take more than a minute or so to complete, deepen the neural pathways of RSF. Remember, neurons that fire together, wire together. By writing down the answers to these questions regularly, you train your brain to think in this manner.

1. What Three Things Did I Do Well in the Previous 24 hours?

The first question in the Success Log forces you to identify three things you have done well each day. This may seem simple, but for most of us, this is something that does not come naturally. The key is to remember that the answer isn't what is important; rather it's training your mind to think about what you are doing well, instead of taking these for granted and completely overlooking them. If you don't *force* yourself to identify what you are doing well, PCT ensures that you focus on what you are *not* doing well.

The first is the most important question in the Success Log because self-confidence is the number one variable for performance. When you learn to recognize what you are doing well, you build your self-confidence, and you are, in essence, working directly to improve your performance. Focusing on your successes is a key component of the RSF mindset. That which we focus on expands (expectancy theory). The more you are focused on what you are doing well, the better you will do. Period.

When you are first getting in the habit of completing your Success Log, you may find yourself struggling to come up with done-wells. This is normal. Remember, recognizing what you do well is *abnormal*. We are designed to focus on our shortcomings (PCT). *Anything* that promotes personal or professional health, even by an inch, counts as a done-well. If you woke up this morning and got out of bed without hitting the snooze button, that is a done-well. If you had a loving, two-minute conversation with your five-year-old, that is a done-well. If you apologized without giving an excuse after arriving late to a meeting, that is a done-well. Don't make the mistake of thinking that your done-wells have to involve huge feats of accomplishment. One of my favorite teachings from Coach John Wooden is that it's the little things done well that lead to greatness. Your done-wells don't have to be huge in order to create a huge impact. When done consistently, focusing on even just one inch of improvement puts you miles ahead of the normal problem-centric way of thinking.

The mere act of evaluation causes improvement.

---

2. On a 10-Point Scale, How Well Did I Do Completing My Professional Process Goal? and 3. On a 10-Point Scale, How Well Did I Do Completing My Personal Process Goal?

Questions two and three in your Success Log ask you to evaluate your success on your two most important activities (personal and professional process goals) on a 1 to 10 scale. This is an essential component of keeping yourself on track. The mere act of evaluation causes improvement. If you have fallen off track completing your process goals, recognizing this in your Success Log lets you get back on track faster. If your personal process goal is to exercise for 30 minutes daily, and you completed your workout that day, you would score a 10. To score a 10 doesn't mean you did the workout perfectly. It merely means you got it done. If your professional process goal was to make 10 proactive phone calls, and you completed 6, you would score a 6. The goal for completing your process goals is to be at a 9 or better consistently. If you have 90 percent completion of your process goals or better, you deserve great results, and you will consistently achieve great results. Anything less than 90 percent on completing your process goals is a guarantee that you are underperforming on your potential. If you are not where you want to be with executing your process goals, the next two questions will help you get on track.

4. What Is One Thing I Want to Improve in the Upcoming 24 Hours?

The highly successful have an *obsession* with improvement. There is a big difference, however, between an obsession with improvement and an obsession with perfection. This is where the fourth question on the Success Log comes in. "What is one thing I want to improve in the upcoming 24 hours?" Notice that you are only looking for *one thing* to work on improving each day. You will be significantly more successful at making positive change if you focus on improving one thing at a time, one inch at a time. Thinking you are tough enough to take on more than that is a mistake. Limit yourself to one improvement daily within your Success Log.

---

*Focus on improving one thing at
a time, one inch at a time.*

---

5. What Is One Action Step I Can Take to Help Make the Improvement?

Identifying what you want to improve within your Success Log gets you only part of the way there. It is easy for most people to recognize *what* they want to do better, but what most people don't do is take the next step of identifying *how* they can make that improvement. The fifth question in the Success Log asks you to use an RSF mindset to figure out one action step toward improvement. "What is one action step I can take that could help make the improvement?" Your answer to this question must involve something actionable and measurable. If you wrote in your Success Log that you want to improve your patience with your kids, a response like, "Try to not get as frustrated with them in the morning before school" won't cut it. At the end of the day, it would be very difficult to determine whether you were successful at this, and telling yourself to "try" doesn't help you get there. My guess is that you are already trying to be successful at whatever it is you are working on improving.

The key is to come up with *something specific to do* to contribute to your success. For example, you might answer, "Lay out all the kids' outfits for school tonight, so we are less rushed and stressed in the morning," or "Every time I feel myself about to raise my voice, take a centering breath." You are then able to easily measure whether you were successful with committing to either of these processes. Did you lay out the kids' clothes? Yes or no? Did you take a centering breath when you felt yourself about to yell? Yes or no? These are much easier processes to measure than "Did I try to x?" or "Did I focus on y?" Now, if whatever you come up with does actually cause an improvement, great! If it doesn't, you can simply try something else the next day if that is still your desired improvement.

Either way, you will be far ahead of where you would be had you stayed on the problem side of the mental chalkboard without searching for solutions. You came up with a potential solution, and that is a win, whether it worked or not. If the same item is still something you want to work on improving the next day, you can include it as your one thing to improve in your Success Log for that day. Some improvements come more easily than others. You may have to try several different solutions before you find one that sticks. It is critical to remember the Plus 1 concept here. Your goal should be to find a way to improve your current situation by one inch. Don't let the entirety perspective take you out of your fight for improvement. If you find yourself writing down and working on the same thing day after day, don't mistake this for a sign of failure. This is a sign of *relentlessness*. You are keeping yourself in the fight, and that is a sure sign of mental toughness.

If you find yourself writing down and working on the same thing day after day, don't mistake this for a sign of failure. This is a sign of relentlessness.

---

6. On a 10-Point Scale, How Well Did I Do with RSF Today?

Question six asks you to rate yourself on a 1 to 10 scale on how well you did with RSF today. Remember the metric for measuring RSF is moving from thinking about a problem to searching for a potential solution within 60 seconds. If you could move from a problem to a solution within 60 seconds about 50 percent of the time, you would be a 5 on the 10-point scale. If you could shift your focus from a problem to a solution within 60 seconds 90 percent of the time that day, you would be a 9 on the 10-point scale. The goal for questions four, five, and six is to be at the 9 or higher range. In my experience, that is where those who are most successful live. Realize that if you are writing down 9s or better on your Success Logs, you are probably behaving in a manner that has you performing at your potential. Think about this for a minute. When have you ever had a method of accurately evaluating if you were performing at or above your potential? Success Logs give you that ability.

Nines or better are the goal; however, just because you aren't there yet doesn't mean you aren't succeeding. Learn to celebrate *all* improvement. If you started at a 4, try to move up to a 5 or better the next day. If you started at a 1, try to move up to a 2. Remember, perfection is not the goal. Improvement is the goal. If you keep your focus on improvement, you will get to a 9. Again, once you hit 9s on a regular basis, you know you are operating at or above potential. Doing so for extended periods of time will undoubtedly improve your results. You will have days when you fall short, but by now, you already know the tool to use to help you move forward—*What is one thing I can do that could help make this better?* The RSF tool will help you win any and all fights.

The RSF tool should become your secret weapon. It is your secret weapon against PCT. It is your secret weapon against underperforming on your most important tasks. It is your secret weapon against remaining stagnant. It is your secret weapon against the times when you will undoubtedly fail. When you find yourself at a loss for what to do, use the RSF tool. When you find yourself winning, use the RSF tool. We cannot overstate the impact of this simple little question: *What is one thing I can do that could help make this better?*

The RSF tool will help you win any and all fights.

The Success Log provides you with a daily practice of applying this question to what you want to improve so that you learn to use it for the unexpected things life throws at you. Waiting until you are feeling mentally weak to use the tools for developing mental toughness and the RSF mindset is like going to get your vaccination after you already have the flu. You will not necessarily feel better when you complete Success Logs. However, be confident you are vaccinating yourself against the negative toll PCT would be causing otherwise. This is why the *daily practice* of completing the Mental Workout and Success Log is so important.

Don't spend more than 90 seconds each day completing your Success Log. Allowing yourself more than 90 seconds makes it likely that you will sit with it for too long trying to be perfect. If you get through only the first question in those 90 seconds, no problem. Start a new one the next day. In this case, done is better than perfect. Spending 90 seconds completing any portion of your Success Log counts as "done." Completing imperfect versions of the Success Log consistently is much better than creating perfect versions inconsistently. Eventually, you will likely get through your Success Log much more quickly than even the 90 seconds, but 90 seconds is the maximum.

Here are Ellen and my Success Logs from the past 24 hours as examples.

Ellen:

1. What three things did I do well in the previous 24 hours?

   Played with the boys outside for an hour instead of putting them in front of the TV

   Went on walk and completed workout

   Wrote for an hour

2. On a 10-point scale, how well did I do completing my professional process goal?

   10

3. On a 10-point scale, how well did I do completing my personal process goal?

   10

4. What is one thing I want to improve in the upcoming 24 hours?

   Connect with Patrick

5. What is one action step I can take to help make the improvement?

   Have a drink with him on the front porch after the kids go to bed

6. On a 10-point scale, how well did I do with RSF today?

   9

Me:

1. What three things did I do well in the previous 24 hours?

Worked out (legs and cardio)

Spent some extra time with a client in need

Sent my wife an "I love you" text

2. On a 10-point scale, how well did I do completing my professional process goal?

5

3. On a 10-point scale, how well did I do completing my personal process goal?

10

4. What is one thing I want to improve in the upcoming 24 hours?

Get back on track with 30 minutes of writing daily

5. What is one action step I can take to help make the improvement?

Move it from 6:30 a.m. to 6:00 a.m. Create time block

with alert.

6. On a 10-point scale, how well did I do with RSF today?

9

You can find the template for the Success Log at relentlesssolutionfocus.com. Make copies of it, and keep the copies where they will be easy to see and fill out. I know we are asking a lot of you in this chapter, but please take 90 seconds right now to complete your Success Log for today.

SUCCESS LOG

1. What three things did I do well in the previous 24 hours?
2. On a 10-point scale, how well did I do completing my professional process goal?
3. On a 10-point scale, how well did I do completing my personal process goal?
4. What is one thing I want to improve in the upcoming 24 hours?
5. What is one action step I can take to help make the improvement?
6. On a 10-point scale, how well did I do with RSF today?

THE 72-HOUR RULE

Your Mental Workout and Success Log are the most comprehensive ways to train your mind to focus and maintain attention on the details that deliver success in your life. Just as your body responds to *consistent* strength training, your mind responds to regular training. Take one minute and 40 seconds *each day* (or at least three days per week) to develop your mental strength and stay in shape for performance by completing your Mental Workout. Take another minute or so (but no longer than 90 seconds) to complete your daily Success Log to make the RSF mindset your new normal and stay ready for adversity when it strikes. Be sensitive to the 72-hour rule. Muscle deterioration begins within 72 hours of your last workout. If you should miss a day here or there, don't panic. One missed appointment with your physical trainer won't sink your overall physical fitness, and the occasional missed Mental Workout or Success Log won't kill your progression to success. Make it a rule to *never* miss three Mental Workouts or Success Logs in a row. If you do miss a couple of days, simply make the commitment to get back on track the following day.

THINGS TO *KNOW*

1. The Mental Workout has been proven—at the highest level of competition—to help individuals develop the RSF mindset.
2. The Success Log teaches individuals to create new neural pathways of thought that are deeply connected to increased health, happiness, and success.
3. Consistently completing the Mental Workout and the Success Log (at least three days weekly for each) is critical to training the RSF mindset. Both can be completed in less than three minutes per day. Remember, neurons that fire together, wire together.

THING TO *DO*

Prioritize Mental Workout and Success Log completion by taking a moment right now to decide exactly when and where completing them fits into your schedule. Yes, these collectively take only about three minutes, but we want you to reserve that time daily on your electronic or paper calendar. When completing your Success Log, be sure to be in a place where you can write down your responses. Make copies of the template provided at relentlesssolutionfocus.com or create your own notebook. Writing down goals has been shown to produce nine times more success than not putting your goals on paper, as researched by professor emeritus at Virginia Tech University, David Kohl. Writing down your Success Logs makes them more impactful.

Next, set a reminder. This could be asking Alexa to tell you every day to complete your Mental Workout and Success Logs, or sticking a Post-it note on your nightstand, or leaving this book wherever you will see it frequently to serve as a constant reminder. This may seem like overkill now, but we can't stress its importance enough. Give yourself the best chance possible to develop the habit of completing your Mental Workout and writing down your Success Log daily. Your health, happiness, and success depend on it.

Now you *know* everything you need to about developing the RSF mindset, and it's time for you to *do* it. Even though the *doing* takes you only three minutes each day, there will be days when you have to force yourself. Committing to these new habits is simple, but that does not mean it will be easy. Putting these reminders and schedules in place makes it easier. You can do this!

Attack 1 Thing

Y ou have read this far; do *not* stop now.

Let's review the three steps to developing mental toughness and the RSF mindset.

Step 1: Recognize. You must be able to RECOGNIZE when your thoughts begin to focus on negativity or problems. The built-in alarm system that alerts you when your mind is moving toward PCT is *negative emotion*. Anytime you experience stress, anxiety, fear, anger, depression, or guilt, that is your cue that your thoughts are on the problem side of your mental chalkboard.

Step 2: Replace. Once you RECOGNIZE that your mind is focused on the negative, you must REPLACE your problem-centric thoughts with solution-focused thinking, ideally within 60 seconds. The simple and incredibly effective method of crossing the line from PCT to RSF is to force yourself to use the RSF tool: *What is one thing I can do that could make this better?* Be *relentless* about always finding a "Plus 1" solution to your problems, specifically when it comes to your two process goals. This enables you to apply RSF to all areas of your life.

Step 3: Retrain. Learning to RECOGNIZE your negative thoughts and then quickly REPLACING the problem focus with an emphasis on solutions dramatically improves by RETRAINING your mind. Mental Workouts and Success Logs done consistently (a minimum of three days weekly) change the neural pathways of your brain so that moving past problems toward solutions not only happens more quickly and efficiently, it becomes your norm.

RSF is the mindset that will allow you to live your life to the fullest. You will know RSF is inside of you when you consistently focus on the strengths in yourself and the good in the world. As we are imperfect beings living in a problem-focused world, you have the awareness that issues will arise, and when they do, you can and will solve them. With consistent completion of your Mental Workout and Success Logs, instead of getting sucked into problems, worry, and negativity, you will more regularly find yourself thinking, *"What is one thing I can do that could make this better?"*

There will be times when you get into a groove with solution-focused thinking, and then there will be times when you find yourself defaulting back to PCT. When that happens, it means one and only one thing—you need to refocus on completing your Mental Workout and Success Logs consistently.

Ellen and I want you to keep a copy of this book in plain sight—on your desk, coffee table, or wherever you will see it throughout the day—and each time you see it, remind yourself to be relentless about finding solutions to any and all of life's problems. Remember, one inch counts. I have always loved Coach Wooden's quote, "It's what you learn after you know it all that counts." You now have the knowledge that gives you an advantage for the rest of your life, if and only if, you do something with it. Remember, knowing something isn't enough—you must do something.

You are worth it.

ACKNOWLEDGMENTS

A deep thank-you to the following for inspiring Ellen and me with your thoughts and actions: Alfonso Soriano, Scott Parker (Barndog), John Wooden, Tom Bartow, Rick and Ellie Scheeler and their children—Paul, Catherine, Bernadette, Bridget, John, and Mary—Bill Belichick, Kye Hawkins, Max Heffernan, Nando Parrado, David Goggins, Martin Seligman, Maxwell Maltz, Bob Gassoff Jr., Tony Christensen, Kelly Hall-Tompkins, Walt Jocketty, and the 2006 and 2011 World Champion St. Louis Cardinals. The contributions to mental toughness you all have made will not soon be forgotten.

A big shout-out to Casey Ebro and the McGraw Hill family for bringing RSF into people's homes and lives.

INDEX

ABOUT THE AUTHORS

Dr. Jason Selk is one of the premier performance coaches in the United States. He helps numerous professional and Olympic athletes, as well as Fortune 500 executives and organizations, develop the mental toughness necessary to outperform the competition and achieve high-level success. While serving as the director of mental training for the St. Louis Cardinals, he helped the team win their first World Series in more than 20 years in 2006 and their second World Series in 2011.

A top speaker, he gives 50 keynote speeches per year. His clients include UBS Financial, Edward Jones, The Capital Group, Ernst and Young, Northwestern Mutual, Enterprise Holdings, Humana, and Miller Brewing Company, as well as athletes in the NFL, NHL, NBA, PGA, LPGA, MLB, and NASCAR. A regular contributor to *Forbes, Inc., Success, Shape*, and *Self* Magazine; ABC, CBS, ESPN, and NBC radio and television, he has been featured in *USA Today*, CNBC, and *Men's Health*.

He is the bestselling author of four books, including *Executive Toughness* and *10-Minute Toughness*.

Dr. Ellen Reed has been a top performance coach for more than 10 years working under Dr. Jason Selk. She has extensive experience in mental training for business, athletics, academia, and the performing arts. In addition to her work helping others reach high-level success, she has a well-established and successful career as a professional dancer. Since 2010, she has been a company member with The Big Muddy Dance Company, which presents premier quality dancing and choreography to St. Louis audiences and beyond. With a background in academia and the performing arts, she helps business leaders, athletes, and students reach their peak performance by developing the mental toughness necessary for success.

She received her doctorate in experimental psychology, with a focus on memory and cognition, from St. Louis University.

For more information, visit jasonselk.com.